Back in Control

Back in Control

MY STORY

TINA MALONE

sphere

SPHERE

First published in Great Britain in 2014 by Sphere

A CIP catalogue record for this book
is available from the British Library.

ISBN: 978-0-7515-5482-3

Typeset in Baskerville by M Rules
Printed and bound in Great Britain by
Clays Ltd, St Ives plc

Papers used by Sphere are from well-managed forests
and other responsible sources.

MIX
Paper from
responsible sources
FSC
www.fsc.org FSC® C104740

Sphere
An imprint of
Little, Brown Book Group
100 Victoria Embankment
London EC4Y 0DY

An Hachette UK Company
www.hachette.co.uk

www.littlebrown.co.uk

Dedicated to . . .

My dad, Frank. I love and miss you dreadfully.

My beautiful Aunty Doreen – never forgotten.

Our Lyn – my rock; always there for me.

My mate Kerry, for your beauty, love and friendship.

My kind, loving, loyal, funny, wonderful, sexy husband –
you changed my life, Paul. I'm lucky to have you.

My beautiful, talented, clever, funny daughter, Dannielle.
I love you more than you will ever know.

My beautiful baby girl, Flame Frances Josephine Malone –
welcome to my world.

And mostly, for everything – loving me constantly –
my mum, Olwyn. I wouldn't be here without you.
Love you, Mum.

Prologue

I stood in front of the mirror in my hotel room taking in the rolls of fat, the big flabby belly. I was enormous. Arms like an all-in wrestler. I sucked in my cheeks. My face was huge and I had no neck. Without even looking, I knew there was a solid hump on my back where the fat had gathered. *Fat, ugly pig.* Disgusted, I put my clothes back on, the same shapeless dress and grey fleece top I'd been wearing for days, turned off the light, sank on to the bed in tears, and lay in the dark, sobbing, hating myself, wishing I was dead.

It was 12 March 2008, and I was in Sharm El Sheikh, in Egypt.

Some holiday it had turned out to be. I'd come away with my daughter, Dannielle, and her best friend Baby Lee, my niece, Michaela, and Richie, one of my closest friends, thinking we'd have a laugh, but almost as soon as we arrived I began to lose the plot. I opened my suitcase in the room I was sharing with Michaela and started crying. The sight of my clothes depressed the life out of me. There was nothing I wanted to wear, not a single thing I felt good in. I wanted to bin the lot. At 19 stone 3 pounds, I was the biggest I'd ever been, wearing horrible, baggy, size 28 clothes. I had been big for years, usually no heavier than around 15 stone, which was bad enough, and while I knew I'd got fatter, I hadn't realized how much weight I'd piled on until I got on the scales before the holiday. It was a horrible wake-up call. At forty-five years of age, I'd become morbidly obese and there was no getting away from the fact my weight was killing me.

The day stretched ahead. The others had gone out. When I'd said I wasn't going with them – again – there'd been murder with Dannielle, who thought I was moping about, feeling sorry for myself. The truth was, I was in the grip of a deep and frightening depression.

I didn't know it, but I was having a breakdown.

For the third day running, filled with self-loathing, I sat in the room eating chocolate and crisps, drinking bottles of water. Hours went by and I thought about maybe going to sit by the pool. At least I could get a bit of sun on my skin. I drew back the curtains from the patio doors and bright sunlight flooded in, making me squint. The pool was right in front of me, a few steps away. Sun beat down on the clear blue water. From where I stood I could see the line of palm trees running the length of the beach. I'd been to Egypt before and loved it, done the sights, gone to Luxor and the Valley of the Kings. Not this time. This time I wasn't going anywhere. The pool was so close. All I had to do was step outside. I told myself it was no biggie, opened the patio doors and felt the heat. Minutes passed as I stood on the threshold thinking about making it as far as the nearest lounger. How many steps was it – a dozen? Twenty? I breathed in the warm air, felt the sun on my face. It would take me thirty seconds, if that. All I had to do was put one foot in front of the other. It was as if my legs were made of lead. Another few minutes went by while my heart raced and my stomach knotted up and panic got hold of me. I could not move. Something inside was holding me back, stopping me from stepping over the threshold, keeping me a prisoner inside the room. In absolute despair, I closed the patio doors and drew the curtains, plunging the room into darkness again.

I couldn't remember ever feeling so utterly pathetic.

After years of struggling with my weight, my eating was out of control. I hated myself and knew I had to do something about it. At the same time, it was as if all the fight had gone out of me. I lay on the bed wishing I was dead, begging to go to sleep and not wake up.

'Please, God, take me,' I said, burying my face in the pillow, tears streaming down my cheeks.

1

I've never been late for anything in my life, apart from my own birth.

When I made my entrance on 30 January 1963, I was three weeks overdue and Mum and Dad were on a day out in Bristol. Mum went into labour as they were about to go on a boat trip. Dad took her to the local hospital instead and, hours later, I was born. According to my mum, I didn't want to come out and had to be pulled and tugged and dragged. Stubborn, even then. No one remembers my exact weight, just that I was a big baby, about 8 pounds. They named me Christina Marie. I was Christina to my dad, Chris to my mum. I was so overdue I can't help wondering what my parents were doing having a day out in Bristol in the first place. You'd think they'd have wanted to stay close to home. Just in case. Years later, I took my mum to task about it and she said things were different back then, there weren't all the scans you get now, and doctors weren't able to be as precise about when you were likely to give birth as they are today. Even so. Thinking about it, maybe it said something about my parents. Even as a child I knew they were unusual. Out of the ordinary, different.

Eccentric, you might say.

My dad, Francis Thomas Patrick Malone – Frank – was one of six children, five boys and a girl, and came from a very middle-class background. His father, John Joseph, was Irish, and his mother, Leonie, was French. Dad went to the best school in Liverpool, the Collegiate, and then to university. He spoke a ridiculous number of languages. We counted them up one day and got to seventeen. When I was about three, he would put foreign words and phrases on the walls and I'd sit there reciting *hello, good morning* and *welcome* in Romanian, French, German, Spanish, Italian, and umpteen other languages. When I was five he was teaching me the alphabet in Greek and Latin. His study was crammed with books, everything from Tolstoy's *War and Peace* and William Golding's *Lord of the Flies*, to Machiavelli's *The Prince* and the collected works of Shakespeare. He played guitar, violin, mandolin, banjo and piano, and his musical tastes ranged from Fats Domino to Vivaldi and the Beatles. He loved American TV sitcoms, shows like *I Love Lucy, Abbott and Costello, Mister Ed*, and something called *Grindl* about the ups and downs of a domestic worker played by Imogene Coca. Grindl was his nickname for me when I was little, but because I couldn't say it properly it ended up Grimble. As a little girl, it seemed to me there was nothing he couldn't do and he made me believe anything was possible.

'You can be anything you want to be, have anything you want, if you work at it, Christina. *Anything*,' he said.

I absolutely adored him.

He was fair haired and blue eyed, tall, good looking and elegant, always in a suit. The night he met my mum he was in a club called the Iron Door, in Liverpool, playing the fruit machine when he hit the jackpot. As the coins thundered into the tray, a crowd gathered and Mum went to see what the fuss was about. Blonde and slim with a look of the actress who starred in the Hitchcock film *The Birds*, Tippi Hedren, Mum caught his eye and he ended up buying her a drink. She was eight years younger than him and intelligent, striking to look at, but nowhere near as well educated as he was. It didn't get in the way of them falling in love.

Olwyn Evans, as Mum then was, also came from a big family, of four girls and three boys. Her parents, Eric and Josephine, were ordinary and working class. I'd often stay at my nan's two-up, two-down in Berbice Road, in the Penny Lane area of Liverpool, while Mum and Dad went on holiday. The things that stick in my mind are loads of people coming and going, the back yard full of clutter and bikes and all sorts, lino on the floor, eating my dinner off my knee because there wasn't a dining table, and sitting with my nan plaiting strips of newspaper for the fire she lit every day before my grandad went to work. Nan was a feisty little Irish woman nicknamed Tiny. She was a devout Catholic with crucifixes on the walls and rosary beads on the door handles. No one was allowed in her front parlour except on Sundays in their church clothes before Mass. She wouldn't stand for bad language and if you stepped out of line she threatened to wash out your mouth with carbolic soap. One of my earliest memories is of my mum's brothers coming home one day with an Alsatian and my nan going mad and yelling at them to get rid of it. I spent a fair bit of time there because once or twice a year my parents went away, just the two of them. I'd sit at the window and wave as they drove off to the airport to spend the weekend somewhere exotic, like Berlin or Paris or Vienna.

I grew up in a big Georgian house in Percy Street in Toxteth, Liverpool. We lived in a flat on the ground floor of number 20, although over the years my dad bought up the rest of the house, bit by bit, until the whole place was ours. It cost a grand total of £4,000, around £40,000 in today's money, although that wouldn't go anywhere near what our old house is now worth. It was on the market not so long ago for £850,000. In the sixties, Toxteth was buzzing, what you'd call eclectic. You got all kinds of people there, some wealthy, some with next to nothing, and lots of immigrants from places like the Caribbean and Africa. It was edgy, proper bohemian. Some of the houses near us had basement shebeens, illegal all-night drinking dens with makeshift bars and DJs playing blues and reggae. At one end of our street there were prostitutes and crackheads and, at the other end, doctors and poets and artistic types. My dad loved it. Since he was older and more worldly, my mum was happy to live wherever he wanted to be.

I started school in 1968. On my first day, Dad drove me to Birchfield Road Juniors, his old school, a few miles away from where we lived, in an area called Edge Lane. I didn't mind the idea of school. In fairness, I didn't know what it meant.

On the way, in the car, the radio was on, something lively with a beat, Dad humming along, me in my new school dress and cardigan. The week before, Mum had taken me to get my feet measured at the Clarks shop and it was the first time I'd worn my shiny new T-bar school shoes and white ankle socks. We pulled up at the gate in a brand new purple Ford Zephyr which, thinking about it, probably caused a bit of a stir. A new car was one thing. A big flashy purple one was really asking for trouble in that part of town, not that I knew it at the time. I skipped into the playground holding my dad's hand. There were lots of kids milling around and streaming into the building. Birchfield Road Juniors was a big school with hundreds of pupils. Dad let go of me.

'Off you go, Christina,' he said.

I grabbed on to his leg. It hadn't dawned on me he was actually planning to leave me there.

'Go on, you'll be fine, Grimble.' He tried to shake me off as other kids streamed past.

I held on tight.

He crouched down. 'You'll love it.'

I wasn't convinced and started crying, clinging on to his trousers.

'It's a lovely school. You'll have a great time,' he said, finally working my grip free.

Funnily enough, it wasn't going to school I was upset about, it was the thought of my dad leaving. Maybe I wasn't sure when, or if, he'd come back. Maybe somewhere deep down I was thinking about being at the window at my nan's and Mum and Dad going off, sometimes for a few days, sometimes longer. When you're little, you don't really understand things like time and separation. Years later, a therapist said I had terrible abandonment issues. By the time my dad got me to let go, I'd managed to crease up his suit trousers, not that he seemed bothered. He dried my eyes, told me to be brave and said he'd see me later. I watched him go and went inside with the other kids.

He was right, I loved school. The headmistress, Mrs Morgan, grey-haired with glasses, was big and imposing, lovely. She always had a word for me. You know those kids, the ones that bring in little presents for the teachers? That was me. Dead keen, always first to put my hand up. I'd scribble away in my exercise book the second we were given something to do. If my English teacher, Mr Thomas, drew a squiggle on the blackboard and told us to use our imaginations and write a story about it, I'd be off, head down, filling the page, oblivious to the fact no one else was writing. I'd look up and everyone would be staring at me as if I was mad. I was the oddball, the misfit, the geeky kid. Before long, I was being picked on. Edge Lane was a poor part of town, big families with not much money living in tenement buildings. Even as a child I knew we weren't hard up. We had nice things. We went on holiday. My mum was forever taking me shopping, putting me in paisley-print dresses and matching cardies and Clarks shoes, while some of my classmates were in hand-me-downs and shoes that were shabby and dropping to bits. Some of the kids I mixed with were dirty. They had nits. And there was me rolling up every day in a car. A new car. God in heaven, a *purple Zephyr*. I got a load of abuse about that. Before long, I got my dad to drop me round the corner from the school in the morning so no one saw us.

Too late.

The bullies had me in their sights.

Walking through the playground I'd get a kick up the backside. One of the boys in my class hit me every day. One of the girls, Patricia Jones, made my life an absolute misery. Day in, day out, she got hold of me and punched me in the stomach, slapped me around the head, kicked me, pulled my hair. She was only tiny and practically swung off my plaits. One day she pulled out a clump of my hair. Patricia lived nearby and had loads of sisters and a scary-looking mum, a big woman with a shock of fluffy white hair, who made me think of one of those troll dolls people used to collect and hang round their necks. For her size, Patricia was ferocious and always had a couple of mean-looking friends with her. She would beat me up for anything. For nothing. I came back to school after one of the holidays with a tan. We'd been to Spain, I think. We often went abroad to places like Morocco and Spain, Romania even. Patricia demanded to know how I'd ended up so brown. I was probably only about seven, but somehow I knew not to say I'd had a fortnight in Lloret de Mar, so I lied and said we'd been to Gronant in Wales, camping. You couldn't get anything past Patricia. She was one of those hard, suspicious kids who'd punch you in the face soon as look at you. She got hold of me in the toilets. As far as she was concerned, no one comes back from a week in Wales the colour I was. Obviously, I'd been *abroad*. It was enough to get me battered. Again. I made the mistake of asking why she was picking on me the whole time. I must have thought I'd be able to talk her round. She found that very funny and the gang she hung about with thought it hilarious, all of them having a right old laugh at my expense. Just so I'd know better than to ask any more stupid questions, Patricia gave me another good thumping.

Like I say, I was keen to learn, a bright child. Bright enough to work out that I had little in common with most of my classmates. It was obvious we had things at home that no one else at school had, like a car and a phone and a colour TV. I remember feeling embarrassed that we had an automatic washing machine when I realized that the people I was mixing with had some sort of twin tub, if they were lucky, or a spin dryer with a hose that went into the sink. I wished we did too. I made some good friends at Birchfield, Jean Gerrard and Jeanette Cook, who lived in terraced houses, two-up, two-down, with a toilet outside and a front parlour you weren't allowed to go in, like my nan's. No phone, no car, a little black-and-white television, a radio. It felt as if we lived in a mansion compared with them.

My friends had things like egg and chips for tea, sausage and chips, beans and chips. Chips with everything. We didn't even have a chip pan. I was mortified. Why couldn't we have a chip pan like everybody else? Both my parents cooked – things with spices, like Moroccan chicken stew. Embarrassing things, basically. My dad would make cole-slaw. *Make* it. He'd be in the kitchen chopping and peeling, Jimi Hendrix on the stereo, or Bach or the Beatles, depending on what kind of mood he was in, garlic stinking the place out. No one I knew had even heard of garlic. We'd have things like spicy chicken with broccoli. Asparagus, avocado. Not that I dared tell anyone, because everyone else was having fish fingers and chips. Tinned peas were about as adventurous as it got for most of my friends when it came to vegetables.

Both my parents worked, Dad as a private investigator, Mum as a tax inspector. A lot of what my dad did was knocking on doors serving writs and summonses. He had an assistant, Nobby Clark, an amazing-looking Jewish man who dressed in black and wore a hat and had his hair in traditional curls. Sometimes Dad took me along when they went on calls. He'd joke that he was a real-life Simon Templar, the detective played by Roger Moore in the TV series *The Saint*, and in fact he did have a look of Roger Moore about him. Me and Nobby were his sidekicks, he used to say. Dad would pull up in the Zephyr at some house and leave the engine running while he went and knocked on the door. Sometimes he'd get told to bugger off. I saw him chased by dogs or sometimes throwing the court papers over a locked gate and shouting, 'You are now served,' before sprinting back to the car and driving off in a hurry. I thought it was dead exciting. My dad was always well off and used to say he could make money in an empty room. I'm the same.

The reason they sent me to Birchfield Road Juniors rather than somewhere closer to where we lived was because it was where Dad went and it was handy for my nan, Leonie, and grandad, John. My parents were still at work when I finished school so I walked to my nan and grandad's house and had my tea there. It was only three streets from Birchfield and took about ten minutes, but I used to dread it. About the same time our bell went, so did the one for the boys at St Sebastian's, the Catholic school on Holly Road. I'd be the only one going their way. If I ran into them I'd get called 'posh' for being at Birchfield, maybe because I was always in nice clothes and new shoes. They'd push me round and give me a slap, empty my school bag. I was being battered at school and again on the way home. It got to the point where I came out of school and ran like mad. Sometimes I'd get to the top of Laburnum Road, in sight of my nan's house at the far end of the street, and feel my stomach knotting up. I used to think if I just kept running I'd make it, then a gang of St Sebastian's boys would come round the corner, heading my way and I knew I'd had it. In fairness, they never hurt me as much as Patricia Jones did.

My nan was tall and slim with an orderly house that smelled of bleach and polish. In the hall, in pride of place, was a picture of the French President, Charles de Gaulle, above a table with one of those heavy old black phones. She'd want to know what I'd done at school, what I'd learnt. We'd watch some TV, then she'd get out her stamp album and we'd go through her collection. If she had any new stamps we'd put them in. Somehow stamps from countries like Peru and Bolivia always seemed more colourful and exciting than ours. I had a good idea where most of the countries were because my dad used to spread out world maps in his study and show me. I'd have my tea at my nan's, a proper cooked meal, something like gammon or minced beef with potatoes and vegetables, which we always ate at the table. Come to think of it, I don't think she had a chip pan either.

Now and then I'd go, 'Nan, those girls have hit me again,' in the hope she might do something to help me. I could be wrong, but I got the feeling she didn't want to know.

Although she was kind, I don't think she fully understood what I was going through and what it was doing to me. All she'd say was I should talk to my teachers or tell my dad. Or stick up for myself.

End of subject.

2

In Percy Street, I spent hours in my bedroom by myself, writing poetry, making lists of places I wanted to visit: Argentina, Chile, Peru, Mexico, Brazil. I was always fascinated by South America. I don't remember ever feeling bored or lonely because there was always something I had to do. I'd play with my dolls, Sophia, Tiny Tears, Francesca and Tippy Tumbles, and make things for my teachers. At school I had a thing about washing my hands and spent ages in the cloakroom, which got me punished with the ruler on my hand or across the back of my legs. I spent hours covering my school books with wallpaper, lining them up in order in my satchel, writing my name over and over in the back of my exercise books until every inch of the page was covered. Everything had to be very particular, done the way I liked it. I had a thing about my pencils and stayed up late endlessly sharpening them, taking great care, concentrating, being precise and neat and organized. It mattered that each pencil was the same length, that they all had identical points and looked *right*. Don't ask me why; I couldn't tell you. It just did. My dad would come up, tell me to go to sleep and put the light off. Once he'd gone I'd sneak out of bed, put the light back on, and get back to my pencils. There was always more to be done, one that wasn't perfect. My dad used to go mad. In the end the only way to stop me was to take the bulb out of my bedroom light.

While I was upstairs in a world of my own, sharpening pencils, downstairs the house was buzzing. When my dad had his friends round, you'd get a Jamaican car mechanic, a bass player from the Royal Liverpool Philharmonic, an exotic-looking woman in Ceylonese traditional dress, and some wild-haired spliff-smoking artist at the table. Mum would dish up an amazing stew, the whisky would come out, and they'd be drinking and talking and playing music for hours.

I was about seven when what I think of now as a time of complete madness began. Night after night I'd scream the house down and my father would come rushing into my bedroom. I'd fling myself at him and cling on, hysterical. He would shush me, settle me down and try and get me to go to sleep, only for the same thing to happen again. I'd be crying and shaking, utterly terrified. My parents had no idea what to do with me. As far as they were concerned, I was either attention-seeking or psychotic. I got very clingy with my dad and if Mum went near him I'd push her away. I started calling her Olwyn. I was prone to losing my temper if I didn't get my own way and would hold my breath and throw myself on the floor or kick doors. Proper tantrums. They called in the doctor, who examined me and couldn't find anything wrong. The disturbed nights carried on and I was sent to an educational psychologist in the hope he would get to the bottom of whatever was making me so distressed. I knew exactly what the problem was, but no one believed me.

I had a ghost. Actually, I had two.

I'd be in my bedroom and a tall, elegant man in a top hat and cloak with a cane would appear at the foot of my bed. Some nights I could make out his face and bushy sideburns; others, all I saw was a gruesome skull. I'd start screaming and my dad would come running. Sometimes the figure disappeared; at other times I could still see him as my dad tried to comfort me. I'd be hysterical, screaming and shaking, pointing at the fella in the top hat, but no one else ever saw him. To me, he was clear and vivid and real. I think my parents thought I was going mad.

I went through a phase of turning on taps and leaving them running. Mum and Dad had these friends, Taff and Judith, who had a couple of kids, and we'd go and stay with them. I'd turn on every tap in the house. When my dad asked me why I was doing it, I said it was because of the woman in the rocking chair in my bedroom, that she'd told me to. My parents were tearing their hair out.

I told the educational psychologist about the man in the top hat and the woman in the rocking chair. He put it down to a vivid imagination, sparked by watching TV programmes like *Dixon of Dock Green*, *Z-Cars* and *Doctor Who*. The sessions I had with him didn't help. I kept on seeing the man in the top hat at the end of my bed and screaming my head off. It drove my parents to distraction. It was worse for my mum because she had to be up earlier than my dad for work. After this had been going on a while, she couldn't take the sleepless nights and ended up having a breakdown that kept her off work for months. I knew she was feeling the strain and that, even without the ghost business, I was hard work, but at the same time I was only young and didn't fully understand how stressful it all must have been for her.

My nan, Josephine, must have died around this time. She was fifty-five. I don't remember anyone sitting me down and telling me she was dead, just my aunty Doreen and uncle Rob coming round one night when I was watching TV in the living room. The doors to my dad's study were open and they were all in there when my mum started to scream. I mean, *scream*. I could see Doreen holding on to her, then my dad came through and told me some story about Aunty Val burning her hand and Mum being upset. I don't know how I worked out my nan was dead, I just somehow knew. It was lung cancer that killed her, even though she'd never smoked.

I was eight when my brother, Simon Peter, was born. I had prayed for a boy and remember running into school to Mrs Morgan and going, 'My mum's had a boy!' To celebrate, I got a brand new blue trouser suit made of Crimplene, which was all the rage: flared pants and a little waistcoat, white socks and slingbacks. With my flares and frilly white blouse and long brown hair I felt like Peter Noone out of Herman's Hermits. I went off to the hospital dressed to the nines to meet the new baby.

I became completely obsessed with my brother. I took him

everywhere with me. The two of us were very close. Before he was born I'd been going to the Lesley Morris Dance School for tap, ballet and jazz classes. Mum used to take me and I loved it. We put on shows and the first time I went on stage was to do a tap number to 'Alexander's Ragtime Band'. I was in orange shorts, a bottle-green top and an orange cap. In the wings waiting to go on, I fainted, went out cold. I don't know what that was about. When I came round, I felt fine, so I went on and did my routine. I loved being on stage, performing, and I wanted to be a dancer. Then, not long after Simon was born, Mum said she was too busy with the baby and couldn't take me any more. I was gutted. It had never crossed my mind that having a little brother would change things and, at first, I resented him, but that didn't last long. In no time at all, I was besotted with him and begging my mother to let me take him out.

Just before Simon was born I stopped seeing the man in the top hat and cape in my bedroom. It ended overnight. Just like that, things went back to normal. I even stopped calling my mum Olwyn.

In the flat above us on Percy Street was a scene painter at the Liverpool Playhouse, Pete Sainty. Pete had wild black hair and a goatee beard and his place was littered with paint-spattered canvases. His girlfriend, Marilyn, had short red punky hair, a bit like Mia Farrow, and slouched around looking dead sexy. Pete and Marilyn loved to throw parties and when I was about eleven my dad decided I should be allowed to go to one. Mum was dead against it but Dad was adamant, determined I'd have all kinds of experiences. I borrowed a mohair sweater from Marilyn and wore a pair of Wranglers I'd taken in to make them proper skinny. Upstairs, Jimi Hendrix belted out of the stereo and there were all these people with long hair smoking big spliffs. Bowls, some with coleslaw and others with some kind of strange beetroot stew, were dotted around. The actor Don Warrington, who played Philip in the TV series *Rising Damp*, was there. Barry Andrews, an actor who was on TV in an advert for salmon paste, also turned up. His was a very familiar face in Liverpool and in our house. Every time he popped up with a fish in the ad, my dad would go, 'There's Barry again!' I was fascinated and impressed and hung about in the background watching all these interesting people.

My parents spoiled me rotten, Dad giving me money, Mum taking me shopping. She was always treating me, getting me new outfits. We'd come home loaded down with bags and it would all be stuff for me: a new coat, a dress that went with it, another dress that didn't, shoes, hotpants, boots. My mother always looked good. Every day of her life she wore heels. Even her slippers had a small heel. When I was little, she wore halter-neck maxi dresses and huge platform shoes. She had a good eye for fashion and knew how to take something ordinary and make it work. When she was a kid and my nan didn't have the money for swimming costumes for her and her big sister, Doreen, Mum decided to cut the sleeves off their Fair Isle sweaters and turn them into bathing suits. They looked the part – until they got into the baths and the wool stretched. Still, it tells you my mum knew how to take a garment and do something clever with it. She'd get little bottles of shoe dye from Timpson's and I'd watch, fascinated, as she spread newspaper on the floor and the bright pink platform heels she was bored with became an eye-catching shade of purple. A plain dress would get the tie-dye treatment. She had a box full of scarves and she'd pull them out and find something that gave an outfit a totally new slant. All the time, she changed her hair. I remember it blonde, dark, red, cropped, wavy, permed. She wore wigs too and had lots of different styles on polystyrene heads in her bedroom.

My dad was always in a suit, navy usually, and a shirt and tie. Even on holiday he'd be in long pants and a white shirt open at the neck. That was about as casual as he got. The only time he succumbed to a pair of shorts was at the hotel swimming pool. Never in a million years would you have persuaded him to wear a pair of jeans or, God in heaven, trainers. No, no, *no*.

Appearances were important to my parents. A lot of the time they were tanned from being on holiday somewhere hot. At home, once the tan faded, they had one of those little sunlamps that were popular for a while, for their faces. Eventually, my dad bought a proper sun bed, the kind they had in salons where you lay down and got brown everywhere. Even when I was small I knew my parents were well-dressed, good-looking people.

I didn't look like either of them.

From about the age of seven I felt different, that no one really understood me. Years later, when I was having therapy, I started to think about what I was like as a little girl – obsessively sharpening my pencils, having night terrors, seeing ghostly figures – and it made me think about how intense I was. Mad Tina. At school, I was desperate to fit in and never did because my home life set me apart, and, at home, half the time I drove my parents crazy. Looking back, I wonder if even as a child I was depressed and my behaviour then was a sign of things to come.

3

In 1974 I started at Blackburne House Grammar School. It was a girls' school, the best in Liverpool, and places were sought after. I had to sit an entrance exam, two two-hour papers, I think. I don't ever remember any discussion at home about what would happen if I didn't get in. It was assumed I would. The exam tested you on English, maths and general knowledge. You had to do an essay. All of us taking the exam sat at desks in rows in a huge hall, scribbling away, teachers walking up and down, saying how much time was left. It was a big deal for an eleven-year-old, the pressure to do well, I suppose, but I didn't find it hard, not in the slightest. I was a kid who'd always loved learning, always done my homework. I was already into books like *Treasure Island, Alice's Adventures in Wonderland, Little Women*, and, thanks to my dad, I knew about writers like Dostoyevsky and Tolstoy. Exams came easily to me. I sailed through.

I was going to a posh school – *the* posh school – and Mum took me into town to get my uniform. The only place that stocked it was the department store George Henry Lee's. If you were shopping for your uniform there, you'd done well. We had a list of stuff to buy, from a gabardine mac to a leotard with the school crest on it. Blackburne House was strict, which meant every single item had to be bang on. It couldn't be any old gym bag, it had to be the *right* gym bag. You couldn't cut corners and get a pleated skirt that was similar but not identical to the one on the list. It had to be the one they said, the expensive one from George Henry Lee's. That's how it was. If you wanted to go to Blackburne House, you did things their way. So there I was in my sensible skirt, white shirt, yellow, green and blue tie, a blazer with the school crest sewn on to the breast pocket by my mum, knee-length socks, sensible flat shoes – every inch a Blackburne House girl. I even had a beret.

It seemed the perfect moment to totally reinvent myself.

At Birchfield Road Juniors I'd been bullied and beaten every single day. Being the keen kid, the one who wanted to learn and got her homework in on time, got me punched and kicked and ridiculed. The biggest lesson I'd learnt from my years at Birchfield was that it wasn't cool to be nice. I wasn't about to make the same mistake again.

At Blackburne House, I became hard and scary, in-your-face. I completely changed. If anyone looked at me I'd be, like, 'What you looking at?' I became a proper scally. I took on bigger girls, stood up to the bullies, got into fights. At the same time, I was popular and funny, the joker, streetwise, the one everyone wanted to hang round with. One thing I wasn't ever going to be was the one that got picked on again and punched, believe you me. Never ever. I'd had more than enough of that. When I first started, a girl in the year above me hit me in the face with a netball. On purpose. I picked up the ball, went over, and smacked her on the back of the head with it. She was livid, up for a fight, ready to put me in my place.

'Right, I'll see you later,' she said.

'OK, see you up by the shop on the corner after school.'

If she thought I was some little dickhead first year, she was about to get a nasty shock. I wasn't scared of her. She was older and bigger, but I didn't give a monkey's. All I was thinking was, *no one's fucking hitting me here*. I wasn't having any of it, not any more.

After school, I went to find her and battered her.

From when I was about ten I'd always gone to an ice rink, the Silver Blades in Kensington, near to where my nan, Leonie, lived. I'd get my dad to drop me off round the corner because I didn't want anyone to know we had a car. I was embarrassed about living in a big house with a phone, but at the same time there was another part of me that loved going to Morocco with my dad and spending a month exploring the markets, or visiting Ceausescu's Romania.

I'd had my first boyfriend when I was about nine. Gary Bates. All dead innocent, playing out in the street, having a kiss and going home for your tea. At that stage, in my bedroom I had posters up of the gymnasts Olga Korbut and Nadia Comaneci, as well as Michael Jackson, Donny Osmond and David Cassidy. I'd go on to my friends about how much I loved David Cassidy. Sex was something I knew nothing about. A couple of years later, once I was spending all my time at the ice rink, things changed, and from about the age of eleven I became very sexually aware. My dad sat me down and did the whole sex-education talk. He was very open and matter-of-fact, using the kind of pictures you'd get in a biology text book to explain how the male and female reproductive systems worked. Periods, abortion, prostitutes – he told me everything.

I was mad on a guy at the rink, Billy Williams, who was a couple of years older than me. I used to sit in my bedroom and fiddle about with bus tickets, put them in a certain order so that the letters that ran along the top of each ticket spelled out BILLY, and sew them all together. *Sew* them. Don't ask me why bus tickets or what that was all about. I couldn't tell you. I even tried to write his name on my arm. With a compass. That's how crazy I was about him. If he sauntered past and gave me a wink I was so overcome I'd practically collapse and all me mates would be going, *He winked at you. Billy Williams winked!*

Billy was blond, blue-eyed and good-looking. He was also a fantastic skater and played for the Liverpool Leopards, the ice hockey team. I'd have killed to catch his eye, but most of the time he totally ignored me. I couldn't work out why he wasn't interested. I was a posh girl from a good home – and a scally as well. I'd have a fight with anyone. Thanks to my mum, I had the best leather gear in the place. And I hadn't shagged everyone like some of the girls had. My dad had taught me not to give myself away. One of the things he liked to say was, 'Bad boys and good boys like *good* girls. Bad boys and good boys *use* bad girls.' It sank in and I made sure I was a good girl. Still, Billy wasn't interested. He'd shoot past on the ice and not give me a second look. Thinking about it, maybe I was a bit too young. The girl he went out with was a *real* scally: hard as nails, proper brassy, lean, looked like she'd fucking kill you. Since Billy didn't want me, I went out with another boy I met at the ice rink, but I couldn't even be bothered walking to the bus stop with him, never mind kissing him. Years later, I was in hospital and a woman visiting someone in the bed next to mine asked me if I'd gone out with so-and-so, that same lad, at the ice rink. Turned out she'd married him and they'd had four sons, all of them heroin addicts.

I'd go skating with my best friends from Blackburne House, Karen Maloney and Kerrin Rodney. Karen was very attractive with long red hair in a flicked-out Farrah Fawcett style and big boobs. I was quite plain, had no boobs, and wanted to be like her. All the boys fancied Karen and I was slightly in her shadow. She was the centre of attention and I felt inferior, like her little clown friend. It bothered me so much I actually wrote her a long letter saying she made me feel stupid and why did she have to speak to me like that in front of boys. It was a sign of how I was that when something got to me, I'd dwell on it for ages. When Karen read the letter she said she had no idea what I was talking about.

Kerrin had long brown hair, same as me, blue eyes and freckles. She was very pretty. Still is. Me and Kerrin wore the same leather jackets, sewed up our Wranglers to make skintight jeans, and had the suede boots and sovereign rings.

My first big love when I was about thirteen was called Mark. He was tall and dark-haired and lived in the tenements down Scotland Road, near where Kerrin lived. For a few months, we were serious. For my birthday he bought me a bottle of Charlie perfume, a key ring with the letter T on it, and the Beatles' *Sgt. Pepper* album. I saw him every night and we talked about what we'd do when we got older, as if we'd still be together. It didn't seem ridiculous at the time, not to us. All we did was kiss. We'd snog for hours and hours, then I'd go home with a big red rash around my mouth, so there was no hiding what I'd been up to. After Mark, I went out with Tony, another Scotty Road lad, who was blond and looked like Kurt Russell. Then I started seeing *another* Mark. All of them serious relationships, by the way, for the few months they lasted. I seem to remember having the shall-we-get-married-when-we're-sixteen chat with more than one of my boyfriends.

Karen was crazy about a guy at the rink, Barry Coy, who played for the ice hockey team and was an incredible skater. Everybody fancied him. He was only a couple of years older than us but was something of an enigma and came across as philosophical, spiritual – and a bit of a bad boy. This was the seventies when the Jackson 5 and *Shaft* were huge and there was Barry, mixed race, gorgeous looking, with his massive afro and long patchwork leather coat, coming across like he was wise and all-knowing. He had it all going for him. I got very matey with his twin, Melvin, and the two of them would come to Percy Street to play pool at my house. For the first time in my life I became aware of racism with people going, 'Doesn't your dad mind two black guys coming to the house?' It was a complete shock to me. I couldn't work out why people thought it mattered what colour your skin was.

I was always into music. When most of my friends were into bands like Sweet and Mud, I was mad on Marvin Gaye, Diana Ross, the Foundations, the Temptations. The first record I bought was 'Build Me Up Buttercup', the Temptations' version. I moved on to Bob Marley, Herbie Hancock, Barry White, Earth, Wind & Fire, Steel Pulse, the Stylistics, Stevie Wonder, Al Jarreau. All my music was black. When Earth, Wind & Fire played Bingley Hall in Stafford in 1974, I was desperate to go, but my parents wouldn't let me. My mum was the type who wouldn't entertain any discussion. Once she said no, that was it. I went anyway with Barry and Melvin Coy on a trip from the ice rink. Coming back, the coach dropped us off at two in the morning and they walked the three miles from the ice rink to Percy Street with me. When I got in, my mum gave me a hiding.

I adored my brother, Simon, and took him with me to the ice rink sometimes. He was blond and blue-eyed, the most gorgeous five-year-old. Because my mum loved clothes, he'd be kitted out in all the latest gear – a full-length Tony Spencer leather jacket and little flares – and everyone thought he was dead cool. When the Liverpool Leopards were playing in some competition, me and Simon went on the supporters' coach to see the game in Deeside. It was probably only about forty minutes away, but it seemed like a big adventure. In the end, we only saw a bit of the game because the puck left the ice and flew into the crowd. Of all the hundreds of spectators, I was the one who got smacked in the head. Of course. I was knocked unconscious and stretchered off. Poor Simon was terrified.

That kind of thing happened to me all the time. My dad

always said I'd find trouble wherever it was, and he was right. If I'm walking down a busy street, two thousand people around me, and a brick falls out of the sky and cracks someone on the skull, I guarantee it's going to be me. At the same time, if it's a pot of gold that lands on someone, that'll be me as well. Good luck and bad luck – both come my way in roughly equal amounts.

As well as my mum constantly buying me clothes, the best of everything, and making sure I looked the bee's knees, my dad was forever giving me money. He'd think nothing of giving me twenty quid if I was off out with my mates. They couldn't believe it. I wanted for nothing. Sometimes it got embarrassing, like when there was a school trip and everyone else was putting money on a card every week to pay for it, and my dad wanted to write a cheque for the lot. I wanted to be the same as everybody else, and remember going ballistic when there was a choice of going to Spain or France with the school and he couldn't understand why I didn't want to do both. I screamed at him.

'Because no one else is going to both, that's why!'

When he insisted I took in a cheque to cover the whole amount in one go, it brought back horrible memories of Birchfield Road Juniors and being the odd one out. Again.

At home, I could earn a fiver for nothing more taxing than making Dad a cup of tea and cheese on toast. I can picture him sitting cross-legged in his silk dressing gown, smoking a Benson & Hedges cigarette, shouting through to the kitchen for me to bring the Branston pickle. I could probably have got an extra fiver for that, thinking about it. I always had money. Always. I think that's why I'm terrible when it comes to spending. I had a mum who was endlessly shopping for clothes and a dad who was overly generous, to the point of being ridiculous, and I inherited both traits.

My mate Karen was spoilt too, but in a completely different way. She was an only child and her parents, Irene and Vince, thought the world of her. On a Sunday morning, Karen could be lying on the sofa in her dressing gown feeling fragile and she'd have her dad running round making toast for her. She never seemed to get into trouble for coming in late. It was a proper eye-opener for me. If I came in late, Mum would be waiting, and she would give me a bloody good hiding. It was nothing for me to get a whack round the head or a punch in the face. She could be very hard, my mum. In fairness, I probably deserved it, coming in hours after I'd been told to. If I was meant to be in at ten o'clock and missed the bus, I'd think I might as well be hung for a sheep as a lamb and roll in at two in the morning. A few hours later, Mum would be dragging me out of bed to do the housework. I'd seen what went on at Karen's, her mum bringing her a cup of tea, going, 'How are you feeling?' My mother's attitude was more, 'Get up, you lazy bastard!' She'd have me hoovering the stairs, all seven flights, and doing the ironing before she'd let me go out. I could have friends who'd come from Scotty Road on the bus, three or four miles away, and me mum would make them wait outside while I finished doing whatever job she'd given me.

You did not mess with my mother.

I knew my dad adored me and my mum bought loads of stuff for me, but they never told me I was pretty or amazing or said I looked nice. They just didn't. My father was never one to throw compliments about anyway, and my mother was very reserved. It wasn't as if they were any different with me to how they were with our Simon, but he was a beautiful child with his white-blond hair and blue eyes and I always felt I wasn't all that attractive, so the way my parents were probably impacted more on me. It astonished me to hear Karen's parents constantly telling her she looked gorgeous, practically bursting with pride when she was done up in her heels and her hair all flicked, ready to go out. They had framed photos of her all over the house, their beautiful precious daughter. My parents were the opposite. There were no pictures of me on the mantelpiece. I don't even remember that many photos being taken. Strange really, since my dad loved gadgets, but never really bothered with cameras. All those amazing holidays we went on and there's no cine film, hardly any photos. I think I've gone the other way to make up for it. On my wedding day, in 2010, I had 4,500 official photos taken.

4

I was more interested in going out and being with my friends than working hard at school. I wasn't the most academic girl at Blackburne House but found I could wing it and still come top in some subjects. I was probably a bit of a nightmare as far as the teachers were concerned, because I was the one with an answer for everything. I was cheeky, I suppose, but that was all. There was no truanting or turning up without your tie or with eyeliner on. They would never have put up with it. When a teacher came into a class, the talking stopped and you stood up. If you had so much as the wrong socks on, your parents would be called in. That's how strict it was. It was like being in the army. I absolutely loved it. The teachers were amazing. I had Miss Reed for English, Miss Lloyd and Mrs Mason for French, Mr Parry for biology, Miss Greenhalge for geography, Miss Eggleton and Miss Engelberg for sport, Miss Arnold for history. Maths was never my best subject and I was in the bottom set with Mr Everett. Mr Taylor, who taught physics and chemistry, was dead strict. If you so much as raised your head when you were meant to be getting on with some written work, he'd chuck the blackboard duster at you. He was a good shot and I got clouted with it a few times. I still see him now, out and about in Liverpool – and I still call him 'sir'.

Ann Bates took us for drama and made a huge and lasting impression. She was a small woman with cropped hair, a big booming voice, and a liking for long cardigans and capes. I was already reading the classics, everything from *Wuthering Heights* to *Jane Eyre*, and she got me into the poetry of Wordsworth and Keats. The first part Ann Bates ever gave me to read was the Nurse in *Romeo and Juliet*, and I complained because the character was a fat old woman. She gave me a withering look and told me to get on with it.

'Use your imagination, Malone.'

She taught Shakespeare in such a way she brought it to life off the page. Her knack for storytelling got you hooked in. It's how I teach Shakespeare to my drama students now, getting them interested in the story, whether it's *Hamlet*, *Macbeth* or whatever, and telling it in a way they can relate to before we even look at the language. The beauty of Shakespeare is that the themes are universal, as relevant today as they were when the plays were first written. I remember seeing the late Gary Olsen at the Everyman in 1995 in a version of *Macbeth* that was set in Sarajevo and done in a kind of *Reservoir Dogs* style and being fascinated.

When I was about fourteen we were in rehearsal for *She Stoops to Conquer*, which was going to be a joint production with the lads from the Institute over the road. I was playing the lead, Kate. At the same time, I was hanging round Scotty Road with my first boyfriend, Mark. A couple of times I said to Mum and Dad I was working on the play and instead went to see Mark and missed a few rehearsals. Ann Bates wasn't happy and pulled me up. I remember saying something about how I knew my lines and was better than half of them that were in it and didn't need to go to all the rehearsals. Words to that effect.

'These have to work at it and I don't,' I said. 'So I've missed a couple of rehearsals, what difference does it make?'

'It's discipline,' she said.

In the end, I didn't do the production and lived to regret it. I really missed out there. 'You're lad-mad, that's the problem,' was my dad's take on things. It wasn't that so much as I wanted to be with my friends *and* do the play and felt pulled in different directions.

Toxteth and all its seediness drew me in. As a teenager, I was street savvy and used it to my advantage. If I wanted a scally lad, I'd stick my suede boots on and my long leather trench coat and pretend I was hard as nails. If I wanted to talk to a nice boy from Mossley Hill, I'd get my beret on, my grey socks, my gabardine mac and my briefcase. I was very good at switching between the two. From the age of fourteen I was drinking and clubbing it in town and was sexually aware but, because my dad had drummed it into me to treat myself with absolute respect and never give myself freely, I had high moral principles and knew I'd be a virgin until I was sixteen. I always had this attitude of, 'I'm no one's for a bag of chips and a half of lager.'

Half my friends were clever and middle class and snobby and the rest were scallies whose idea of doing well was finding a footballer or the best criminal around – one with a Ford Capri, preferably – and getting a ring on their finger by the time they were sixteen. It was a strange mix. There was a period during my teens when part of me desperately wanted to be in the crowd with the leather trench coats, Fruit of the Loom jeans, suede boots and sovereign rings, hair in a wedge cut, short at the back, long fringe over one eye, hanging on the corner drinking cans of lager and smoking ciggies. I played at being a scally until I almost became one. Years later, I came across a quotation from Cary Grant that summed me up: 'I pretended to be somebody I wasn't until I became that person.'

That was me, exactly.

There was never a dull moment in Toxteth. One night my mum and dad were parking the car in the back entry behind the house when two guys with crowbars appeared. One of them grabbed my mother, who screamed the place down. I was inside with Simon and we heard all the commotion and ran to the window. My dad threw a punch and hit one of the blokes but they got his wallet and ran off. Another time, the old guy who lived next door was mugged on his way in after a night at the pub. He'd had a few drinks and was an easy target. We found him on our doorstep bleeding from a stab wound.

I got badly beaten up one day outside the chippy next to the Rialto at the end of our street. It was early, about five o'clock, and the girl who attacked me was a well-known nutter; nobody wanted to mess with her. I was about fourteen, in my

Blackburne House uniform, and had a kid from our street, Donna, who was eight, with me. The nutter was a couple of years older than I was and had two of her mates with her. I was about to go in the chippy when they told me to hand over my money. I said no, knowing that wouldn't be the end of it. I got in the queue and waited my turn. Outside, the nutter and her mates hung about. I'd been in a few fights, but this was one girl I didn't want to take on. She would kill me. I was a regular in the chippy, in there every week getting fish and chips for my parents, so I asked if I could use the phone and call home. They wouldn't let me. Gradually, the queue went down and the nutty girl was still outside, arms folded, waiting. I paid for the fish and chips, gave them to Donna, and told her to run as fast as she could and get my dad. She took off across Parliament Street. There were still people in the shop and I thought one of them would help if it all kicked off. I went outside. The nutter and her mates followed, poking me, pulling my hair. I turned round and told them to leave me alone. That got me a punch in the face. One of the other girls jumped on my back and I was dragged to the ground. They were kicking and hitting me and I couldn't do a thing about it. Not one person came out of the chippy to help. A black lad coming down the road on his bike dragged them off and I ran, battered, covered in cuts and bruises, all the way home. The girl who attacked me ended up a crack whore and in jail for stabbing a punter to death so, thinking back, I got off lightly.

It was round about then me and Kerrin started working weekends at the Holiday Inn on Paradise Street. Kerrin's mum, Sarah, who managed the restaurant, got us in. In the seventies, the Holiday Inn was *the* hotel in Liverpool. Marvin Gaye stayed there. Dr Hook. Prince Charles. All the footballers were regulars, so we'd be serving pre-match breakfasts to the Liverpool and Everton first teams. It was good money, £7 a shift, I think, and we made loads on tips. We also earned a few extra quid babysitting for the players' kids, Kerrin mainly for Kenny Dalglish and his wife, me for an Everton player, John Gidman and his wife, Claire, who had a little boy, Patrick.

We probably seemed older than we were, more like eighteen than fourteen. I'd done a fair bit of travelling and been brought up around food and drink that wasn't what you'd call run of the mill, so no one was going to faze me asking for Earl Grey tea or whatever. We'd finish our shift and go to the pub and have a few drinks with the chefs. Half a lager and black. Gin and tonic. That was where the drinking started.

We liked to dance and liked to drink, me and Kerrin, and we started going out clubbing, moving away from the Scotty Road boys to flashy clubs like the Continental and Snobs, where the footballers went. Kerrin's mum was dressy and glamorous with long, jet-black hair and a liking for diamonds and fox furs. She always looked amazing. We wanted to be like her, so we'd get dressed up to the nines to go out. I knew when I put on a tight dress and a push-up bra and went to Snobs that men were interested, but we were never promiscuous. We were proper snotty Blackburne House girls, earning good money at the Holiday Inn, and splashing it on stylish clothes. Admittedly, a lot of the stuff came from the shoplifters on Scotland Road – grafters, they were called. You'd pay £30 for a £200 dress. I had a long purple skirt and a matching batwing-sleeve top with little diamantes in a lovely crepe material. I felt beautiful in it, like a film star. I also had a floral-print dress that nipped in at the waist and cost a bomb. Or should have, if I'd had to pay full price. We even had little fox-fur jackets we'd saved up for, me and Kerrin. Her mum wore Elizabeth Arden make-up in toasty beige, so we did too. I think the whole of Liverpool did. When it came to lippy, it was always bright red.

We used to spend ages getting ready, in her bedroom or mine, listening to the Stylistics, getting through a bottle of Martini or gin before we went out. When I moved from the attic into a different bedroom at Percy Street, my mum discovered loads of empties under the bed and smacked me. If my parents caught me and Kerrin in the kitchen putting on make-up, getting ready to go out at ten or eleven at night, they'd ground me, but it was such a big house we'd wait until they were in bed and sneak out anyway.

We got to know all the clubs and we could get in any of them because the doormen knew us from the Holiday Inn. The only place that had all-nighters was the Babaloo, the most popular club in town, where people queued for hours to get in. The music was hard-core funkadelic and inside it was a seething mass of afros, everyone dancing. The couple who ran it were Jake Abraham and his wife, Marie. Their son, also called Jake, became an actor and, years later, he and I worked together. He was my husband in the film *Blonde Fist*, and then on stage in *Guiding Star* at the National Theatre.

Me and Kerrin went to clubs like the Sierra Leone, where you knocked at three in the morning and it was up to the doorman whether you got in, and the Shangri-La, which was all black guys and white women. We had some great nights out and always knew where to find a shebeen in some dark, dingy cellar with a fella on the decks, maybe a guy playing bongos, sawdust on the floor and a makeshift bar. Some of those places were earthy, raw, and attracted some dubious people, but we went for the music and because you could always get a drink.

We loved a drink.

The south side of Liverpool, the Toxteth side of town, where the music was predominantly black and it was a mixed crowd, was very different to the north, where black people didn't go. The north side was Irish and Catholic. Big families. Sovereign rings and sheepskin coats. In those neighbour-hoods you scrubbed your step and kept your place spotless, wore your best togs to church on Sunday, and had a pan of stew on the stove. You hid your poverty – like my nan, Josephine. If someone knocked on your door in Scotland Road you gave them food, even if you had nothing, even if it meant you went without. That was the mentality.

You didn't have to stray far to get into trouble. One night me and Kerrin ventured out of Scotty Road to go to a disco a couple of miles away and got chased by about twenty girls. Somehow, they knew we went to Blackburne House. That was bad enough, but they also knew I was from Toxteth which, round there, might as well have been another coun-try, and started yelling, calling me black. We took off and jumped on a bus. If they'd caught us they'd have battered us. There was always violence, horrible fights kicking off. A friend of mine lived near Breck Road and we'd see running battles on the dual carriageway between gangs of lads armed to the teeth with pickaxes, bricks and bottles. A lot of people carried Stanley knives and there were loads of stabbings. I always remember being in Caesar's, a club in Wood Street, when a black guy was stabbed to death. It was massive news in Toxteth. By then, I'd seen it all – guys using hammers and pool cues in fights, a lad sat next to me in the pub having his face slashed open – but for someone to lose their life was rare and it sent shockwaves through the city.

5

When I was about fourteen, the fat began to kick in. Not that I was paranoid about my weight. I was quite happy, as far as I remember. I was a size 12 and didn't feel fat. It was my mum and her sisters that had the problem. Doreen, Olwyn, Val and Astrid were all very thin and very beautiful and determined to stay that way. My mum always watched what she ate. She had a thing about her height, which was why she always wore a heel. According to her, if you were short you looked dumpy, even if you were a skinny size 8. Even now, my mother is traumatized if she goes up to 9 stone after a holiday. I mean, proper traumatized. Won't eat. And she's seventy-four. Still, I didn't grow up thinking food was a big deal. We ate well, with our broccoli and asparagus and my dad's spicy chicken or Mum's lamb stew, but food was never the be-all and end-all. My parents didn't even eat out that much. They were never bothered about restaurants. Music and holidays and making the house look nice were always more important to them.

I never had a complex about food and was never a greedy pig when I was younger. That came later. OK, I liked my chocolate and crisps, same as my friends did, but you'd never have said I was a kid who loved my food or raided the fridge looking for something to eat. That just wasn't me.

My aunty Doreen, who was also my godmother, got me wondering if I was overweight. I was staying with her when my mum and dad were away somewhere and she forced a tablespoon of cider vinegar down me every morning 'to break down the fat inside my body'. It got me thinking. Was I fat? Did I need to lose weight? Maybe she knew something I didn't. All I kept hearing from then on was, 'You're too fat, Chris.'

What's interesting is that my mum and her sisters all had girls – Lynn and Carol, me, Susan, Angela and Jackie – and at one time or another we've all had issues with our weight, either piling it on or getting too thin.

A shopping trip sticks in my mind, Aunty Doreen taking me and our Carol to get outfits for the wedding of Mum's eldest brother, Eric. We went to Chelsea Girl and tried on loads of stuff. I ended up with a skirt and, to go with it, a blouse that fastened up the side. I thought it looked all right until I heard Doreen on the phone to my mum saying she couldn't believe how fat me and Carol were. It was only when I got older that I thought maybe it wasn't so much that we were fat, more that my mum and her sisters were incredibly thin.

When I was fifteen I developed terrible stomach pains, so

bad I was admitted to Myrtle Street Children's Hospital. They kept me in for a week under observation, ran various tests, and decided there was nothing wrong with me and sent me home. I'd been home two days when I woke up with the worst pain I'd ever had. God in heaven, it was terrible. I screamed the house down and my mum came running. My father was out, in Manchester, having a night at the dog track. I was in absolute agony. Mum phoned for an ambulance and got Simon out of bed. He was about eight, poor kid, and was frightened to death seeing me in such a state. The ambulance crew stretchered me out, back to Myrtle Street. I barely remember the journey with the siren going, me screaming in agony, Mum and Simon bouncing around in the back of the ambulance as it sped through red lights to the hospital. It turned out I had every reason to make a fuss.

My appendix had burst.

I was in terrible pain and taken straight to theatre. Being wheeled in was a bit of a blur, although one thing stuck in my mind and that was the voice of the man who was going to operate on me.

'This child's enormous,' he said. 'How am I going to get through that fat? Look at the size of her around the stomach.'

It was the last thing I heard before I went under the anaesthetic and the first thing I remembered when I came round after the operation. It had a profound impact on me. *This child's enormous*. I'd just had major emergency surgery, dozens of stitches, but it was what he'd said that most upset me. I didn't tell anyone about it. I was too embarrassed. For weeks, I was in hospital, really poorly, recovering. I remember being weighed, feeling anxious about getting on the scales, and being told I was 9 stone 2 pounds, which didn't seem that enormous to me.

After the operation I was left with a bit of a belly, what I call a shelf, and I wondered if the surgery had something to do with it. Even before I piled weight on later in life, I could never get rid of my belly, not even when I went through a phase of being really skinny.

I couldn't tell you who operated on me but I'll never forget his words or the disgust in his voice and how he made me feel. I suppose coming on top of the cider-vinegar treatment, the shopping trip to Chelsea Girl, being told the whole time I was fat, and my parents never telling me I looked nice, it got me thinking. I knew I was utterly spoilt materially; I knew that my dad drumming it into me from being a small child that I could do anything and be anything I wanted as long as I worked hard enough had given me huge confidence. At the same time I looked at my best mates, Karen and Kerrin, two very different but beautiful girls, and I guess there was a part of me that felt like the ugly one.

I was desperate for my mum and dad to tell me I looked nice but it never came. At times I felt as if they didn't see me. I came home one day with my dark hair cut from a bob into a wedge and dyed blonde with streaks. Neither of my parents said anything for about three hours. They didn't notice. The one thing it did for me, growing up like that, and I only realized this later on, was, as I got older, it made me so I didn't give two fucks who did and who didn't like me. I'm the same now, immune to what other people think. It really, genuinely doesn't matter to me. My daughter's the opposite and we've had rows about it for years because if she hears or reads something nasty about me, she takes it to heart. I don't. I go, are they paying my mortgage? Are they sleeping with me? If the answer's no, I'm really not arsed.

I was fifteen and drinking in the Dolphin pub with Karen and another mate, Sonia, when I met Alan. He had black hair and big brown eyes and he was the most beautiful thing I'd ever seen. I'll be honest, I always liked good-looking men, always punched well above my weight. When he came over and asked if he could buy me a drink, I nearly fell off my chair. He was a bit older than me, about twenty, and doing some kind of apprenticeship, training to be a welder, I think. He came from a big family and I could see he was impressed when I told him I lived in Percy Street in one of the big houses. When he asked how old I was, I said eighteen. He asked if he could take me for a drink the next night and we made plans to meet up. I can remember having to drag myself away because it was a school night and I had to be in at a reasonable time. Not that I told him, obviously. I think I made something up about having to run to get the last bus home.

I went out with Alan for something like five or six months and it felt like five or six years. He came to the house and we sat in my dad's study holding hands watching the telly. I was never allowed to take him up to my room. He was lovely, very quiet, and I was crazy about him. I made up my mind that I was going to save myself for him. He was the man I was going to sleep with. He'd met my parents and I knew he really liked me, but I never met his family because he knew his dad wouldn't approve.

It was all going well until one night we were sitting in the living room with my mum and she was flicking through a catalogue and made some remark about school. Whatever she said gave the game away that I wasn't in the last year of sixth form, which was what I'd told Alan. He looked at me and I felt sick, knowing I'd been caught out. At the door when he was leaving he asked how old I really was and I came clean. Fifteen.

'I can't see you any more,' he said.

That was it. The man I was saving myself for turned and walked away. I was in bits. For about two weeks solid I sat in my room playing Rose Royce 'Love Don't Live Here Any More', over and over, sobbing, hysterical. My first big love had finished with me. It felt as if my life was as good as over. Every night Kerrin, Karen and Sonia came round while I cried my eyes out. It was like a wake.

Two weeks later one of Alan's best friends, Paul Crombie, asked me out. I was obviously feeling better by then because I said yes. It must be something you give off that tells guys you're not the kind of girl they can meet and ten minutes later be wanting to take home. They always knew if they wanted to see me, they had to do things properly. We ended up going out for a few weeks and he came round and met my parents. Paul was a chirpier character than Alan and from a good Catholic family. My dad wasn't too keen on me seeing anyone, but he was OK with Paul, who came across as a hard worker, on a market stall with his dad and his brothers, planning on going to university to study architecture. Or so he said. Things were never serious with him and when he dumped me I can't say I was upset.

I didn't see Alan again for years, then I bumped into him when I was out one night. I was with someone and so was he, but I asked him round to Percy Street. Mum and Dad were away on holiday and I cooked his tea and we watched some big football game on the telly, Liverpool against Roma in the 1984 European Cup Final, I think. Liverpool won on penalties anyway. He said he'd really liked me, that I was from a good family and he couldn't believe his luck. Then, when he realized how old I was, that was it. Over. We started getting it on and then both kind of pulled away, awkward. I guess we'd missed our moment and it didn't feel right any more.

That was the last time I saw him.

6

I left school at sixteen with seven O levels. My dad, who'd had high hopes for me and wanted me to stay on, then go to university, was devastated. I'd made up my mind, though, and there was no talking me round. I might not have been the most academic girl at Blackburne House, but I did manage at least one honour before I left. Up until my final year it was the teachers who picked the Head Girl but, in 1979, they decided to let the pupils vote for whoever they wanted. It was a bold move, really. Past Head Girls had been bright and brainy, academic high-flyers, like Edwina Currie. I don't suppose for one second anyone thought I'd get voted in, since I was hardly what you'd call ideal Head Girl material, but I proved the popular choice. Tina Malone – Head Girl!

In the fifth year, we all had a session with a careers advisor, a bloke in a suit and thick glasses with greased-back hair and lots of information on everything from studying medicine and law to teacher training – the kind of stuff you'd expect to be of interest to a Blackburne House girl. I already had a pretty good idea of what I wanted to do after two years of working weekends, serving breakfasts at the Holiday Inn. When the careers advisor asked what I intended to do with my life, I told him I had experience of hotel work and that I'd probably go into catering in some shape or form. I'd already looked into going full-time in the restaurant at the hotel on £50 a week, which was a lot of money for a sixteen-year-old in 1979. With tips, which were always good, I could make double that.

He nodded. 'And is that all you're interested in – hotel work?'

Actually, there was something else, something I'd been thinking about but hadn't mentioned to anyone. Still, he was the careers man, so now might be the time. I took a breath. 'To be honest with you, no, it's not the only thing … I was thinking I'd love to become an actress.'

He seemed a bit surprised and waited for me to go on.

'I'd like to try for the Royal Academy of Dramatic Arts in London but I don't really know how to go about it so I wondered – have you got any information?'

He sat back in his chair and laughed. Something had obviously struck him as dead funny. 'It's never going to happen,' he said, still laughing. Obviously, what was funny was me saying I wanted to go to RADA.

I won't pretend that RADA was a long-held dream, but something about those drama lessons with Ann Bates had made a massive impact. I loved standing up, doing the

speeches from *Hamlet* and *Romeo and Juliet*, using my imagination. Acting came naturally to me. What I'd been through
at Birchfield Road Juniors, getting bullied for being keen and
coming from a nice home, had taught me it wasn't safe to be
myself – not if that meant being the odd one out. At
Blackburne House I'd played the part of the hard girl, the
scally no one dared have a go at, and it worked. I was equally
at home in a posh club like Snobs drinking champagne with
footballers as I was in a grubby shebeen in Toxteth. I could
switch from one to the other at the drop of a hat, which
seemed to me what you did as an actor. So, all things considered, it didn't seem totally mad to think about a career in
acting.

Not to me, anyway.

The careers officer was still chuckling. 'No, stick to your
hotel catering,' he said, riffling through a pile of papers.
'There's a form here for a course you could do to get some
skills.' He pushed it across the desk.

I thought, yeah, you're probably right, took the form and
went. The idea of becoming an actress got put in an imagi-
nary box and filed away out of sight for the next five years.

When I wasn't working at the Holiday Inn I was out clubbing, mixing with what my father called low substance. I
stayed out all hours, drinking. I'd be on cider and black, lager
and black, Cherry B and cider, Martini. If I went out for
something to eat, a Chinese or an Indian, I'd be on the wine,
Mateus Rosé, and think I was posh. My mum would still
smack me for coming in late while my dad absolutely
despaired. After making me believe I could be anything I
wanted, I don't suppose coming in drunk night after night

was what he'd had in mind. When we argued he'd say, 'Why do this, Christina? Why push me away? Why push away everything I teach you that's good in life? What's happened to you? You've become impressed with clothes and money. You'll get married to a criminal just to annoy me.'

Then I met Jimmy.

I was close to our Susan and Carol, who were my cousins but had always been more like sisters, and we'd go to clubs like Tiffany's and the Harrington Bar. There was a gang of us girls and lads that hung round together. Jimmy Cullen was one of the lads, two or three years older than me, and in a gang called the Lawrence Road Lunatics. That probably should have told me all I needed to know. He was blond with a long fringe over one eye, which was the look in 1980. He wore a red leather box jacket and could dance, really dance. The kind of music being played then was Ultravox, Adam and the Ants and Dexy's Midnight Runners. Jimmy had something cool going on, a way of talking that was hip and proper. Women were falling over themselves to be with him. Everyone fancied him, except me.

I hated him.

He hated me, too.

I'd be done up to the nines, a face full of Elizabeth Arden make-up, red lippy, fox-fur jacket, and he'd be going, *Who do you think you are? How come you think you're better than everyone else?* And I'd be going, *Because I am.* It drove him mad. For a while, I went out with one of his mates, who turned out to be an armed robber, so that was the end of that.

One night, walking home, Jimmy was going the same way

because he lived at the top of Parliament Street, not far from Percy Street. I was with one of my mates and he was with one of his and the two of us argued all the way until he grabbed me and the next thing we were kissing. We started seeing each other and I fell hook, line and sinker. I was completely, madly in love. Once you got him away from the peer pressure of his gang, Jimmy was a nice guy, funny. The bottom line, though, was he was a bad boy who got into trouble, so it was no surprise when he ended up on remand in Belle Vale for violent behaviour and affray, stupid drunken stuff. The fact he was locked up didn't put me off, not in the slightest, and I went to visit him.

'Do you want to get engaged?' he said. 'Shall we get married?'

Not the most romantic proposal in the world and definitely not the loveliest setting, but I was a kid, seventeen, and ecstatic. The next day I was out looking at wedding dresses.

When he was released, I slept with him. Then he finished with me. I was devastated. I'd imagined a wedding, the two of us setting up home, a happy ending, basically, and he didn't want to know. He'd used me.

I carried on working at the Holiday Inn, clubbing with my mates and our Carol and Susan. Then I started throwing up in the mornings. I was so sick. I did a pregnancy test. Negative. The sickness carried on. I did another test. Negative, again. I wasn't reassured. Never mind what the test said, I knew I was pregnant and I was terrified, not that it ever crossed my mind I wouldn't go through with it. I went to see Jimmy and told him. It's hard to know what I expected, but maybe even then I thought he'd want me back, that he'd say we'd get a flat and he'd look after me, all that. Instead, he went crazy.

'It's not mine. You've been with someone else! You were with someone when I was in prison!' On and on he went, shouting and screaming. I was terrified. That night, I could see why he called himself a Lawrence Road Lunatic.

It was garbage, of course. Jimmy was the only one I'd been with and there wasn't a shadow of a doubt that the baby was his. He didn't want to know, that was the problem. What was weird was he started telling people we'd never been together. Having got on the phone from prison to tell his parents we were getting married, all of a sudden he started saying he didn't even know me. He was in complete denial and horrible with it.

I didn't have a clue what was going on. I'd always gone out with guys who'd treated me well, taken me out on dates, bought me presents. Guys I wasn't having sex with had treated me like a princess. It made me think if you sleep with someone he'll treat you like shit. At seventeen years old I worked out that you should never let a man think you're a sure thing.

For a while, I kept the fact I was pregnant quiet, although Kerrin, who worked with me at the Holiday Inn and saw me being sick the whole time, had a pretty good idea. I was still out partying and drinking. The first person I told was our Simon. I woke him up early one morning when I was getting ready for the five o'clock breakfast shift at work. Poor kid was only eleven and bleary-eyed, and there was me going, 'I'm pregnant!' All he could think was that once my parents found out he'd be in trouble for keeping it quiet.

I tried telling our Susan as well. We'd been to the fair and were walking down Wellington Street, Susan in a striped T-shirt, me in a Fred Perry top, both of us in Fruit of the Loom jeans. When I told her, she was horrified and put both hands over her ears. 'Don't tell me – I'll get battered as well!' she said.

I didn't dare tell my parents. In the end, I got my friend Karen to do it. By then I was more than three months gone. Karen phoned my dad.

'Frank, your Tina's here and she's pregnant and she wants me to tell you because she's too frightened.'

She handed me the phone.

'Get home now,' my dad said.

I got a cab back from Karen's house in the Dingle. All the way to Percy Street I dreaded facing my parents. The only good thing was I knew my mum wouldn't hit me because I was pregnant. I loved the house in Percy Street but that night it felt big and dark and foreboding. Mum and Dad were in the living room, telly off, grim-faced, ready for a showdown. My dad was utterly devastated. He had never met Jimmy but he knew about him, that he'd been in prison, and was appalled I'd ever got involved. I sat there while my dad said he'd have to think about what to do, decide what was best. What I might have wanted didn't come into it. Jimmy didn't enter into it at all. His name wasn't even mentioned. Not once did my dad ask what was happening there or what he had to say about anything. As far as he was concerned, Jimmy Cullen was irrelevant. Whatever was going to happen next was going to be my dad's decision.

Not for a moment did I think he would send me away.

7

I didn't get to have a say. It was all decided for me. I would go into a home, a place in Warrington, and stay there until I'd had my baby, which would then be adopted. Once the arrangements were made, I more or less disappeared off the face of the earth. Hardly anyone knew what was really going on, where I was, or that I was pregnant, such was my dad's determination to draw a veil over the mess he thought I'd made of my life. I couldn't simply vanish, so a story was concocted about me going to Brighton to do a typing course. Even my friends and close members of the family were kept in the dark. Now, looking back, it seems incredible that I did as I was told and meekly went along with the arrangements, just like that, but I did. It was about respect, really, feeling that my parents knew better than I did and who was I to argue?

I was about four months pregnant when I left Liverpool, in

May 1981. It was a sunny day and I had a royal-blue cotton smock dress on. I knew nothing about Waverley House, where I'd be spending the next few months, only that it was a Catholic-run home for unmarried young girls who'd got into trouble. All I could think was that I must be a complete disgrace for my parents to shunt me off and lie to everybody about where I was and what was really going on.

Warrington isn't that far from Liverpool, twenty miles or so, but it might as well have been on the other side of the world. That was how it felt as my dad drove me there, neither of us speaking, my head full of questions I didn't dare ask.

Waverley House was a big old place with lovely gardens, lots of trees and greenery. Dad dropped me off and a woman called Anita Chung, who was effectively going to be my keeper while I was there, showed me where I'd be sleeping. I was in a dormitory with six beds. A couple of other girls who'd had their babies were getting ready to leave and I was going to be on my own. It felt bizarre, as if I'd stepped into a time warp.

I had to keep reminding myself it was 1981, not 1951.

Something about Anita Chung made me think of the governess in the film *The King and I*. It might have been the way she looked, how she wore her hair in a bun, or maybe it was because she was serious and proper and all stiff-upper-lip. If I was crying, she wasn't the type to give me a hug. She was kind to me, though. After I'd been there a few weeks she was going to London to visit her family and took me with her. We stayed in St John's Wood overnight and went to Madame Tussaud's and had a lovely day out.

The routine at Waverley House was that Anita would

shout for me to get up at eight in the morning and I'd get dressed and go downstairs for breakfast. Afterwards, I'd wash the dishes, make my bed and do a bit of tidying up, not that there was much to be done since I was the only girl there. I'd read, have a walk in the garden, go down the road and over the bridge to the little shop to buy sweets and cigarettes, come back, read a bit more. I spent a lot of time in the day room watching TV, sitting on my own surrounded by rows of empty chairs, wondering what on earth I was doing there.

While I was at Waverley House, the riots kicked off in Toxteth, in July 1981. Trouble flared after the police made an arrest and over the next few days there were pitched battles in the streets. Bricks and bottles and petrol bombs were thrown, buildings set alight, cars torched, shops looted. CS gas was used for the first time on the British mainland. I sat in the TV room on my own watching it on the news – lines of police officers with riot shields strung across Parliament Street, fires raging. It seemed a world away. Over the road from where we lived in Percy Street, the Rialto, the old ball-room where the Beatles once played, burned down. Dozens of buildings were so badly damaged they had to be demolished. My parents were told to move out and went to stay with my nan Leonie and grandad John in Kensington for a few nights. Our house survived unscathed, but some people lost their homes. Over nine days, there were five hundred arrests, hundreds of police officers were injured, and the damage to property was put at £11 million. They were never race riots, as some people claimed, but an eruption of simmering tensions between the police and the local community.

When Wimbledon was on I watched every single game

and sobbed when Chris Evert won the women's singles. On 29 July 1981, I tuned in along with millions of other people to watch the wedding of Prince Charles and Lady Diana at St Paul's Cathedral. Sometimes, I sneaked back to Liverpool on the train. I'd meet Jimmy's sister, Debbie, at Edge Hill station and we'd wander round for a couple of hours, then I'd get the train back.

Only a handful of people knew where I was or that I was pregnant. One of them was John Gidman as well as his wife, Claire. Claire Gidman was willowy and beautiful and classy and kind. Because she counted on me to babysit for her son, Patrick, I felt I had to warn her that I was leaving. Of course, she wanted to know where I was going. When I told her I was pregnant and being sent to a home for unmarried mothers and that the plan was for me to have the baby, give it up for adoption, and then carry on with my life as if nothing had happened, she was bewildered. Like me, she probably hadn't realized such places still existed – not that they would for much longer. In 1981, Waverley House was coming to the end of its life, which was why I was the only girl in there. Claire came to see me, rolling up like a film star in a flashy green sports car. She couldn't get her head around me sleeping in a dorm and spending hours alone in the depressing day room surrounded by empty chairs. She kept saying, 'My God – isn't there anything you can do?' There wasn't. My dad had put his foot down and, even at eighteen years old – an adult – I felt utterly helpless to defy him. Claire came again with her husband, and tipped off another of the Everton players, Gary Stanley, who had stayed at the Holiday Inn when he joined the club from Chelsea. One day Gary and his girlfriend turned up in some over-the-top monster of a car with the kind of engine that throbbed and rumbled and shook the building. I was touched they'd made the effort and been so lovely to me. It meant a lot.

They were the only visitors I got, other than my mum.

It never crossed my mind I could leave Waverley House if I wanted to. I wouldn't have known where to go and, anyway, I didn't feel I could go against my dad. He used to drive my mum up to visit me but never came in. I knew he wanted what was best for me, didn't want me to be an unmarried mother, didn't want Jimmy on the scene, to the extent he was ready to write a cheque to make him go away if he ever came knocking. Not that there was much chance of that, since Jimmy was back inside by then. When Mum visited she'd sit and chat about the tennis or what the weather was doing or something she'd seen on telly, nothing deep, never anything to do with the baby. That was a taboo subject, even though every time she saw me I was bigger. I didn't bother with maternity clothes, and when I got to the point my jeans gaped open because I couldn't do the zip up any more, I threaded laces through to keep them up. I ended up huge, yet no mention was ever made of my bump.

Night after night I lay in my narrow bed in the dormitory with its bare walls and sobbed. You read every day about people getting maimed and shot and murdered and abused and I told myself that what I was going through was nowhere near as bad but, oh my God, the pain of being in that home was horrendous. I was lonely and isolated and all I could think about was that I was expected to give my baby away. No one bothered to ask me how I felt about any of it. As time went on, I got more and more attached to the baby growing inside me. I was convinced I was having a boy and for hours I sat and watched him kick and move around inside my belly. It was incredible, absolutely mesmerizing. Sometimes, in bed, I'd throw back the covers and balance a saucer on my stomach or a plastic cup just for the fun of watching him kick and dislodge it. There was no one to share any of it with, just me and my baby. I knew what had been decided for me, what my dad wanted, what I was expected to do.

At the same time I knew how I felt.

On Tuesday 6 October 1981, I was at Warrington General Hospital for an antenatal appointment when my waters broke. I wasn't frightened at the thought of giving birth, probably because I didn't know what to expect once I went into labour. I'd only been to one antenatal class about six weeks earlier and I'd not read any baby books or talked to anyone about it. Anita, lovely as she was, couldn't help there, as she didn't have children of her own. No one had sat me down and told me what would happen, what labour felt like, under what circumstances they might have to do an episiotomy or an emergency Caesarean. I must have got wind from somewhere that an epidural was good for the pain because I asked if I could have one, but the anaesthetist was only available on a Thursday. After my waters broke, I went out and had a ciggie and then they put me in a little room on my own. The nurse pointed at a bell beside my bed.

'When your contractions get closer and the pain gets worse, ring the bell and we'll take you into the delivery room.'

I knew nothing about contractions. 'How close? How will I know?'

She nodded at a clock on the wall in front of me. 'Count them and once they're every five minutes, let us know.'

For the next few hours I stared at the clock and counted my contractions like I'd been told. At first they were fifteen minutes apart. I had no birthing partner, no one to hold my hand. At lunchtime someone brought a corned beef sandwich in on a tray and told me not to eat it. I was starving so, once she'd gone, I had it. Then the pain started getting bad and the contractions were closer together. A nurse came in and had a look at me. 'You're five centimetres dilated,' she said.

I was none the wiser. 'What does that mean?'

'You need to be ten centimetres to deliver.'

'How will I know when it's time to push?'

She looked at me. 'Believe me, you'll know.'

Honest to God, the pain was bad, excruciating. They hooked me up to a monitor and left me to it. I was howling so much a nurse came back in with gas and air. As soon as I had it, I was sick everywhere. She was furious. It was the corned beef sandwich, apparently, the one I'd been told not to eat. I got a telling-off for that. I was in absolute agony and wanted to get up and move around, thinking I'd feel better if I walked up and down a bit, but the nurse wouldn't let me. She told me I had to stay on the bed. I tried everything I could think of to get some relief, pitching about, pulling my legs up and hugging my knees. I had hold of the back of the bed and she slapped my hand and snapped at me.

'Don't be so dramatic, you're not on a film set. There are plenty other women going through much worse than you.'

It might have been my imagination, but I felt as if the

nursing staff knew my circumstances, that I was *one of those* girls – on my own, no partner, no one there for me. I was a Waverley House girl – and they all knew what that meant. I could have been wrong, but at the time it seemed that was why they were being so horrible.

I was told to roll on to my side and, without telling me what she was doing, the nurse tried to get a shot of pethidine in my bum. I jumped and the needle came out. She tried again and the same thing happened, so she gave up. It was too late for pain relief anyway by then, and I was wheeled into the delivery room, desperate to push, being told not to. The nurses were in a huddle with the doctor, whispering about the baby stressing, not wanting to come out. Someone said something about forceps. I'd heard that forceps could dent the baby's head and I wasn't having any of it. I screamed my head off.

'*Noooooooo!*'

They put my legs in stirrups and, even though I'd been told not to, I pushed as hard as I could. The baby came out in a rush and straight off it was screaming, just like its mother. It was 6.50 p.m. and I'd been in labour almost eight hours. I was crying with relief, going, 'What's he like?' They handed me my baby, a tiny sticky creature covered in mess and goo. *He* was a beautiful baby girl: 5 pounds 6 ounces. She went straight for my boob and one eye opened and looked right at me. I cradled her, sobbing my heart out. I'd torn myself giving birth and needed stitches, but I didn't care. All I could think was that I'd done it, I'd had my baby.

It was the best feeling in the world.

I named her Dannielle after a character in the David Essex

film *Stardust*. I decided on a double *n* to make it a bit unusual. The other girls' names I liked were Francesca and Havel. That's right, Havel, out of a book I'd read, a Catherine Cookson, I seem to remember. Dannielle has since said that if I'd called her Havel she'd never have forgiven me.

Since everybody thought I was on a typing course in Brighton, I got no cards, no flowers, no phone calls, not a single *It's a girl* balloon. None of the usual paraphernalia that goes with giving birth. My hospital room was completely bare. My mum came to visit me and when Dannielle cried she picked her up, but I could see there was that bit of distance, a veil that kept her just that little bit apart from her grandchild. It wasn't that she was being cold, more that if she allowed her feelings to surface and the tears to come, I'm not sure she'd ever have stopped crying.

I phoned our Lynn and Carol and they came to see me and bumped into my mum as she was leaving. She was embarrassed because no one was supposed to know where I really was and she didn't know what to say to them. Five days later, Mum was back to pick me up. Dad was outside in the car. It was freezing and I got dressed and put on a denim skirt, grey crew-neck jumper, black tights and burgundy boots. I remember the skirt was a size 12 and I was able to zip it up. I handed Dannielle to the nurse. Leaving her behind was horrendous and, all the way home in the car, I sobbed. No one said anything. As far as my parents were concerned, that was it. I'd had my baby and in a few weeks she'd be adopted. Now things could start getting back to normal. I didn't argue about it. When we got to Percy Street my dad showed me what he'd done to my bedroom, the new carpet and bed, the mahogany suite. I think he hoped that doing up my room would help me get over what I'd been through in the last few months.

Dannielle had a reflux problem and a trapped valve that meant she projectile-vomited everywhere, so instead of going into foster care, which had been the plan, she went to Alder Hey Hospital. I visited her all the time and took her out, went to see Jimmy's parents, Elsie and Danny. At home, I said nothing and my parents had no idea I was seeing Dannielle. I acted the part of a girl who was giving up her baby. No one suspected a thing. This went on for six weeks until I was due to sign the adoption papers. The day before, I went to my mum and told her I'd been seeing Dannielle and that I was keeping her. From the look on her face it was obvious she'd had no inkling. She told me to speak to my dad.

I went and knocked on the study door. 'Dad, I need to tell you something. I want to keep my baby.'

He was in no mood for a discussion. 'You keep it, you leave this house,' he said.

'Right, I'll go tomorrow, then.'

I told the woman from Social Services I'd changed my mind about the adoption. She said it was too late, she'd already found parents, and I had to sign the papers. I said I didn't care, I wasn't signing anything. I was keeping my baby.

I phoned my aunty Doreen and told her. We'd always been close and it was no secret she favoured me. I don't know what was said, what conversations went on in the family, but it was decided I'd go to live with my aunty Astrid in Southport. She had four kids so she probably had less space than anyone, but it put some distance between me and my parents and that was probably no bad thing at the time. The next day I moved out of Percy Street and went to live in Aunty Astrid's parlour. I had nothing, no baby things. Dannielle slept in my suitcase. It didn't matter, though, because I had my daughter and I was ecstatic.

I didn't speak to my father for nearly a year.

8

In Southport, I was obsessed with losing weight and went through a phase where all I ate were dried apricots and prunes. I got really skinny and ended up a tiny size 8. I don't know what that was about, really – a reaction to getting so big when I was pregnant, I guess. I got a job in a shop, went on a few dates, saw a lovely guy called Tony for a while, and had an absolute ball clubbing it and getting pissed and generally doing what most nineteen-year-olds do. I loved being thin. I was always a dresser and I'd buy clothes off the local shoplifters and look the bee's knees.

Looking back, it seemed like it was hot and sunny all the way through the summer of 1982. Dannielle was always in the paddling pool in Astrid's back garden or a group of us would pile in the back of a camper van and go to a lake called Tabby Nook, near Chorley, and jump in off the rocks to cool off. I'd get in with Dannielle, who must have been about eight or nine months old. Someone was always being chucked in, usually our Angela, Astrid's daughter, who was a few years younger than me, or their Jack Russell. It's only recently I've discovered there's a whirlpool in that lake and it's not safe. You wouldn't get me near it now.

I don't know what it was like at home in Percy Street for my mum and dad. Mum would come to Southport to see me and Dannielle and sometimes she'd give me a cheque from Dad. I was so angry with him I ripped a few of them up, even though I could have done with the money. Without a shadow of a doubt, everything, from me being sent to Waverley House and being told I'd have to give up my baby, to ending up living at my aunt's, was down to him. I knew my dad. My mum might have been the one doing the bawling and slapping and hitting, but what my dad said went. It didn't matter how much I told myself he'd only done what he thought was best for me, the fact was he'd sent me away and wanted to get rid of my baby.

I wasn't sure I'd ever forgive him.

At first, he didn't come near, and then he started driving Mum up to Astrid's and dropping her off, not that he ever came in. Thinking about it, the way things were must have put a strain on him and Mum. I know it was killing her, seeing so little of Dannielle, the thought of me sleeping on a couch in Astrid's parlour when that vast bedroom of mine in Percy Street was empty. The breakthrough came when I had to go somewhere one day and Mum said she'd look after Dannielle for me, and it ended up that Mum, Dad, Simon, my nan, Leonie, and grandad, John, took her. Dannielle was about nine months old by then, the most beautiful child. It was the first time my dad had seen his granddaughter and she must have made an impression because a few weeks later he drove up to Southport.

'Get your stuff, you're coming home,' he said.

Just like that, things between us went back to normal. Nothing had changed, in spite of what had gone on. Deep down, I knew he had wanted what was best for me and that nothing he'd done had been with any malice, and the anger I'd felt towards him disappeared.

I'd been back in Percy Street a few months when my mum walked out. Bang, she was gone. It was horrendous, completely out of the blue. I was so wrapped up in Dannielle I didn't see it coming, didn't pick up on so much as a hint of trouble. If anything, I thought my mum and dad were solid, well suited. You never heard rows, only laughter. They'd always been the kind to embarrass you by turning up at school parents' evenings holding hands, letting everyone see they loved each other. For as long as I could remember, Mum had a keyring with a picture of my dad on it and he had one of her. Not me or our Simon, mind, each other. I was a bit put out about it, to be honest. They were always off on some holiday or other, coming back tanned and glowing and full of what a great time they'd had. When it came to decorating, you'd find the pair of them up ladders working away. They did everything together. Financially, they were well off, with a lovely home in Percy Street and enough money to have bought a second home in Florida. They loved it that I was back and Dannielle was in their lives. Basically, they had the good life. I really thought they were happy.

When Mum left, the house fell apart. Dad became so dour

and bent over and grief-stricken, you could almost feel the misery seeping out of the walls around him. It was awful, the kind of miserable atmosphere you were desperate to get away from. I used to call it 'hell house on the top of the hill' after an old black-and-white film I'd seen. My dad was in a bad way, devastated. I watched him crumble, go completely to pieces. He had always been a big, strong man and all of a sudden he was broken, on Valium and Ativan, crying, not coping. I didn't know what was going on, why my mother had gone. Whatever it was, it was between the two of them. After a few weeks she came back, but it was obvious things weren't right. It wasn't laughter you heard coming from the bedroom any more, it was raised voices. A few weeks later, she left again.

My dad became very bitter. Mum wanted me and Dannielle to go and live with her, but I couldn't leave him the state he was in. Then he turned on me. I guess he had to take his anger out on somebody and I was first in line. It became difficult to be around him, almost impossible. All his anger and hurt came my way and I got the blame for my mother going.

'This is all your fault, you've ruined everything,' he said.

In his head, it seemed to come down to me getting pregnant, causing loads of trouble. That was what he said, anyway, and there was probably some truth in it. What I'd done may well have fractured things between him and my mum.

For years, I'd been my father's daughter, like him in so many ways. All of a sudden everything changed. He called me vile names, things I could never repeat. He was hurting, shattered, constantly lashing out, and I bore the brunt of it. He was all over the place, one day crying, saying he couldn't live without my mother, the next calling her all the names and having a go at me for not scrubbing the house from top to bottom. He swung from one extreme to the next.

'You're just like your mother, no interest in domesticity!'

'She was amazing, working all the hours God sent, bringing up two kids.'

'She's no good and you're just like her!'

I never knew what mood I'd find him in from one moment to the next. I was back doing shifts at the Holiday Inn and couldn't wait to go to work to escape the name-calling. It was hard enough anyway having a job, bringing up Dannielle and trying to stick by Dad, while he ranted and raved and called me fit to burn. This went on for about a year, Mum getting on at me as well, wanting to know why I didn't leave him and live with her. It was hard being pulled in two different directions.

Meanwhile, Simon was an angry, disruptive thirteen-year-old going off the rails. With hindsight, what was going on at home was probably a lot harder for him to deal with. The grammar schools were closing and he found himself shunted out of the all-boys Institute, one of the best schools in Liverpool, and into Paddington Comprehensive. Paddy Comp, as it was known, was mixed and not exactly up there with the best in terms of academic excellence. Simon was like me, naturally bright, and changing schools hit him hard. He'd been a posh boy at the Institute and now he was having to fight to survive. Any thoughts of studying and doing well in his exams went by the board.

The first Christmas after Mum went, I was making dinner, turkey and all the trimmings, before going to work in the restaurant at the Holiday Inn. Dannielle was in her playpen, Simon was out on his new BMX bike, and Dad was in a bad way, going on about Mum leaving. My brother came running in to say there was a dead body in the back yard and when I went and looked, sure enough, there was a naked woman – a prostitute, I assumed, from the tattoos on her backside – face down in the entry. That was Toxteth for you. I phoned the local police station, which was round the corner, in Hope Street. They didn't seem all that bothered. An hour went by before a copper turned up, casual, like there was no emergency. I stopped stirring the gravy and took him outside to show him the body. Within ten minutes the place was taped off, crawling with police. Major crime scene.

We sat down for our dinner. I'd done my best but, in fairness, it didn't look much like what Mum used to serve. Dad pushed his food round the plate before breaking down. My brother cut into a sprout, and found a maggot. He threw his knife and fork down in disgust.

'You can't cook like Mum. This is shit,' he said.

I'd had enough. I put my coat on. 'I'm going to work,' I said, 'and, by the way, the baby needs changing.'

Dannielle's father, Jimmy, was out of the picture. His parents, Danny and Elsie, were phenomenal, though, and got me through some tough times, babysitting and helping out. If Jimmy was there when I called round with Dannielle, he'd be banging and slamming doors, being vile, telling his folks not to let me in. They lived not far from us, on an estate that was a world away from Percy Street, and came from the same put-up and shut-up generation as my nan and grandad, Josephine and Eric. As long as your husband gave you his wages on a Friday, you stayed married and got on with it, whatever else went on. They were good, decent people.

Dannielle was the most beautiful child. She was tiny and full of smiles, and from the time she started to talk she never shut up, ever. I used to say she could talk a glass eye to sleep. I was besotted and saved up to buy her lovely things from a shop called Oilily in Cavern Walk. I thought nothing of spending £70 on a tiny pair of jeans, £40 on a little top to go with them, while I got myself a dress for a tenner from Dorothy Perkins. I took pictures of her constantly, every day of her life. I pawned my jewellery to have photos taken of her, that's how bad it was. She did a bit of modelling and I thought I'd get her on the books of an agency. I went to some seedy office in London and handed over £180. Needless to say, that was the last I saw of it.

After a hellish couple of years of my dad going on at me, telling me to decide whose camp I was in, his or my mum's, I couldn't take it any more. I went to live with my mum in Brookdale Road. That went down well, as you can imagine. Now I was siding with Nasty Alice, as my dad had started calling Mum, reverting to type. I was *just like her*. Blah, blah, blah. I couldn't do right for wrong. The bizarre thing was I became the catalyst for the two of them getting back on good terms. Whenever I saw Dad he slipped me a few quid to help out with Dannielle, and if I said Mum was skint he'd give me £100 for her. She was always happy to take it. 'You don't refuse anything except blows,' she'd say. When he pulled up at the house to drop me off, she'd go out and thank him for the money. Soon, he was coming in for a coffee. Before long, he was staying for his tea. It got to the point where he was there every day. He used to say he didn't want her back, but I didn't believe him.

It was obvious he never stopped loving her.

9

I still had mates in Southport and would go up there at the weekend sometimes. I was on the train one day, with Dannielle, when I heard a familiar voice.

'Malone! I see you have a child.'

Coming towards me was Ann Bates, my old drama teacher from Blackburne House, looking exactly as she had the last time I'd seen her. Short, cropped hair, mad-looking cape flapping. She gave me one of her long, searing looks.

'You should have been an actress, stuck at it.'

Everyone in the carriage was listening. It was hard not to, what with that deep, theatrical voice of hers.

'You were bloody good. You could have done something. What a waste of a life.'

I felt like saying, Hang on, I'm only twenty-two – my life's not over yet!

Since my session with the careers advisor in 1979, I'd

never given acting another thought. I'd had my hands full, for one thing. Running into Ann Bates got me thinking, and when I got home I mentioned it to my mum. It turned out her best friend, Maureen Ashley, who was a second god-mother to me after my aunty Doreen, had a nephew, Marcus, who was involved in some kind of theatre-in-education scheme.

'I'll get his number and you can speak to him,' Mum said.

Marcus put me on to the Rathbone Theatre Company in Liverpool, and told me I'd have to audition. I didn't really understand what an audition entailed, but off I went anyway to the Old Bill in Westminster Road, a pub that had been turned into a theatre-cum-studio. I'd dressed up in a pink leather suit, skirt and jacket, fancy boots and sovereign rings. I was plastered in Elizabeth Arden make-up and bright red lippy, and still had my hair in a wedge cut. Proper brassy scally girl. When I walked in and saw the others waiting to audition, I nearly passed out. There was a girl called Louise in a long Gothic cloak, a red curly afro and earrings – one through her eyebrow and another through her lip. Next to her was a guy called Declan in a black shirt and pants and a beret. We all said hello. God only knows what they must have made of me. I might as well have landed from another planet. That old, familiar feeling of being the odd one out surfaced. Just as I was wondering what the fuck I was doing there, a door opened and a bloke with blond spiky hair dressed in a black mohair jumper and jeans came out. Like Sting from the Police, only better looking. Peter Ward was MD of the Rathbone, and he was doing the auditions. I fol-lowed him into the office and sat down.

'So, what pieces have you brought?' he said.

I looked at him. Pieces of what? 'I'm sorry, I . . . '

He tried again. 'Were you thinking of doing something classic or contemporary – or one of each?'

I had no idea what he was on about.

'Your monologues,' he said.

No, still no idea.

'Your audition pieces.'

I'd done no preparation and brought nothing with me. The thought never crossed my mind. I started to tell him about myself instead, saying I'd done a bit of drama at school and thought about RADA but when I told the careers man he laughed at me, then I got pregnant and had a child and went to live in Southport, and now I was back in Liverpool and my daughter was at school and I was working at the Holiday Inn and doing bar work at night. I finally stopped talking and he asked why I wanted to be an actress. I said it was something I'd wanted to do when I was younger but put it aside for years. With Dannielle, I didn't see how I could go to drama school now.

He told me how the Rathbone worked, that they had twenty-eight places and something like four hundred people had applied. If I got in it would be full-time for a year on £56 a week. He said he'd let me know. Oh well, I thought, that's that, then. Two weeks later he called to say I was in. I couldn't say for sure what he saw in me, but I came to real-ize that Peter Ward was very much about giving people a chance, no matter what their background or experience.

My life was about to change.

*

In the twelve months I was at the Rathbone I learned about everything from producing and directing to set-building, scripting and performing. We devised shows and toured all over the north-west, doing two, sometimes three performances a day. Our audiences were sometimes terminally ill children in hospices, sometimes pensioners. We played to drug addicts at drop-in centres and the criminally insane at Ashworth high security hospital. It was the most amazing training and I loved it. I got to work with the elderly and infirm, people who had disabilities, behavioural problems, mental-health issues. Through the Rathbone, I mixed with the kind of people that until then I'd had no experience of, and had my eyes opened to parts of the community I hadn't known a thing about. I ditched the sovereign rings and the charm bracelets, stopped playing the scally, and started being myself. Out went the leather suits and in came leggings and mohair jumpers. The Rathbone was highly regarded and lots of actors had started out there, including Cathy Tyson, Craig Charles and Mark Monaghan. I got to meet phenomenal writers like Willy Russell, Alan Bleasdale and Jimmy McGovern, and did a couple of fringe productions at the Unity Theatre.

Peter Ward was like a god to me.

I was working hard and playing hard. Drinking hard, as well. I liked a binge drink, liked a spliff. I dabbled in drugs, whatever was going, never anything serious. A few years before, I had tried LSD with a friend from Southport. We were in some club in Liverpool off our heads and I started hallucinating. Every time someone flicked ash off the end of their cigarette, it seemed to become a ball of flame. I got jumpy and kept talking garbage, trying to tell people to watch out for all these flames shooting into the air, but no one else seemed bothered. It was only hours later when the effects of the acid wore off that I realized the flames weren't real. God only knows what was going on in my friend's head. At one point she tried to take all her clothes off in the middle of the club. I wasn't too out of it to know that was a bad idea and managed to stop her. I can't remember why, but for some reason we had her mum with us. Thankfully, she didn't pick up on our strange behaviour, even when, at the end of the night, we got into a cab and my friend flipped and tried to shove her mother out into the road. At the Rathbone, I tried LSD again and didn't enjoy it. It made me feel paranoid and insecure. One of my friends had a really bad time and ended up in Sefton Park wanting to top himself. It was horrific. I never went near it again.

I had a few flings at the Rathbone and made some wonderful friends, among them Mickey Jones, who went on to play Lance Powell in *Brookside* and now directs *Coronation Street*. He adored Dannielle and she loved him to bits. The first time she met him she said, 'Are you a girl or a boy?'

He said, 'I'm anything you want me to be.'

He used to pick her up from school and taught her all the songs from *Chitty Chitty Bang Bang* and *Mary Poppins*. He was a huge influence in her life and nicknamed her Dandy. We called him Mickey Poppins. He liked it so much he changed his name. It didn't work once he started directing, though, and needed to be taken seriously, and he eventually changed it back to Jones.

Wendy Harris, one of the directors at the Rathbone, also

became a good friend. She was sharing a flat in Patterdale Road and whenever I went round they'd be making lentil stew or cooking something with pasta and drinking red wine. It was like a throwback to my dad and growing up in Percy Street. When the bedsit downstairs came up for rent, she tipped me off. It had a main room for living and sleeping, a kitchen and bathroom. By then, I'd been living at my mum's a while and wanted some space for me and Dannielle. It seemed a good time to move on. I said I'd take it.

For Dannielle's fourth birthday in 1985 we'd got a Staffordshire bull terrier puppy, a white one. We called him Rooney. He was a proper pedigree and I'd paid something ridiculous like £500 for him. We only had him six weeks when he got pinched out of my mum's back yard. Dannielle was heartbroken, so I went to the *Echo* and asked if they'd do a story to try and get him back. When they said no, I staged a sit-in on the steps of the building and told them I wasn't going anywhere until they put something in the paper. They printed a picture of me and a sad-faced Dannielle with an appeal for Rooney's safe return. It was no good, we never got him back.

After a few months, I got another Staff from a rescue centre, a black brindle bitch called Kelly. When we moved into Patterdale Road she came with us. I had two hamsters, Pip and Squeak, so they came too. It was cramped and Dannielle and I shared a single bed. The £56 a week I was on from the Rathbone didn't go far and money was tight. Many a night I sat with fifty pence to my name trying to decide whether to put it in the leckie meter or buy a couple of fags. Dannielle had started at the fee-paying McKee, a school of speech and drama, in Allerton, which I could never have afforded without my dad's help. Come what may, she went off every morning in her bowler hat and gabardine mac, immaculate, even if I'd been up half the night washing her clothes by hand because I didn't have enough money for the meter to put the machine on.

I was drinking too much and putting on weight. If I tried on a dress and asked my dad whether it made me look fat, he'd say, 'Of course it does. It's not the dress. You'd look fat in anything because you *are* fat.'

As I got bigger, he'd go, 'Bloody hell, you're enormous.'

Not one to mince his words, my dad. He thought there was no excuse. Getting fat was about being greedy, as far as he was concerned. He hated seeing me piling on the pounds and so did my mum, who was never overweight.

The one drawback with the Rathbone was that you could only do twelve months and when my time was up I had to leave. I was distraught. Back I went to the Holiday Inn.

Once you'd been away a year, you could reapply to the Rathbone and I did, auditioned, and got in again. That year, 1986, they took two shows to Edinburgh to the Fringe and I was in both of them. *Abominable Aloysius* was for kids and I played a character called Mowgin in a big blue furry costume. In the other show, *Masquerade*, we wore green silk tops and billowing Arabian-style pants and moved in sync with one another on stage. We had three amazing weeks there, long hard days, two shows a day at the Tick Tock Theatre, and it was phenomenal. My God, Peter Ward would have you out leafleting in the street in the pouring rain, drumming up an audience. We stayed in a dormitory in a hostel and my

mum came up with Dannielle for a few days and stayed in a
hotel nearby, which was great.

I saw as many other shows as I could with my best mate
from the Rathbone, Gaynor. Some were good, some were
crap. We saw *The Cranks*, where three guys playing fugitives
ran round doing physical theatre. We went to a performance of *Dead Marilyn*, where a guy in a coffin was done up as
a zombie version of Marilyn Monroe, which was controversial at the time. We also saw the Cosh Theatre, which
was mostly mime. What those guys could do with their
bodies was mind-blowing, absolutely amazing. We sat in awe
as they walked on the ceiling. We often had to walk miles
back to the hostel at the end of the night because we were
skint.

Peter Ward was such an influence. Back in Liverpool, he
suggested I audition for the panto at the Unity Theatre and
I got the part of the genie in *Arabian Nights*, which brought me
to the attention of one of the most powerful casting directors
in Liverpool, Dorothy Andrew, not that I realized at the time.
Peter pushed me to see as many productions as I could. I saw
Vanessa Redgrave in *Antony and Cleopatra* at Clwyd, in North
Wales, and Glen Walford's production of *Tosca* at the
Everyman, in Liverpool. I took Dannielle with me, wanting
her to experience everything.

I'd had my name on the Liverpool Housing Trust waiting
list and in 1986 they offered me a two-bedroom flat in Toxteth. It had high ceilings and huge windows, loads of space.
You could have fit my old bedsit into the living room. The
rent was low, something like £11.50 a week. It was in a great
spot too, in Huskisson Street, across from Percy Street where

I'd grown up. When I looked out the window, there was my old house, although my dad wasn't there any more. He'd sold up and moved to Anfield.

So, I was back where I belonged, in Toxteth, which was even more eclectic and crazy than before.

10

I was working hard to get on, always rushing from one place to another, doing auditions, plays at the Unity for no money, taking every opportunity I could. I'd either have the flat in Huskisson Street very neat or it would be complete chaos with books and clothes and stuff all over. Never anything in between. When I moved in, my dad had carpeted the place in grey and my mum got me a pink suite. I saw one or other of my parents most days. Dad would walk in, take in the mess and, in this very dry way he had, say, 'Oh, you've been burgled, then?' Or, 'I see the binmen have started delivering.'

I'd be, like, 'Dad, have you got that fifty quid? I need to go now and I need you to run me to London Road to the rehearsal room, then come back and mind Dannielle – you'll have to pick her up from dance over at Penny Lane – and the dog needs feeding . . . '

He'd stand in the middle of the clutter, surveying the chaos, shaking his head. 'Are you regressing, Christina?'

I was happy living in Huskisson Street. It was a great house. I got friendly with the girl who lived next door, Mandy Smith, who had a daughter about Dannielle's age and was a radio presenter with the BBC. The guy upstairs was in a band called the La's, and Ed downstairs, a student, made patterns on the walls from cigarette butts. That was a bit strange, to be honest. Then there was me, up-and-coming actress that I was. We had some phenomenal summers in the back yard, Bobby Brown and Soul II Soul's 'Back to Life' blaring through the open windows.

Another friend, an actor, John Hart, lived in a flat in the house next door and I saw a lot of him. One day, he was round at mine, Dannielle was out, and a mate and her husband turned up. We were all sitting in the living room, chatting, when, without any discussion, this friend of mine started getting a load of heroin paraphernalia out of her bag and fastening a strap around her arm as if it was the most normal thing in the world. I caught John's eye. His jaw was almost on the floor. Neither of us said anything.

'Oh, do you want some?' my friend said.

I shook my head. 'Er, no, I'm fine, thanks.' My voice sounded high, strained. I cleared my throat. 'Anyone fancy some tea?'

I got up and went into the kitchen. John followed me in and shut the door behind him. We had a frantic, whispered conversation and decided the best thing to do was act casual. We made cups of tea and went back into the living room where my mate's husband was now about to shoot up. It was bizarre, surreal. There was a lot of heroin around at the time; not around me, though. I didn't mix with smackheads. At least, I thought I didn't. I sat, drinking my tea, talking about whatever came into my head, burbling on about nothing. John asked if I'd like more tea. I said yes, OK. We were both acting extra polite, nonchalant, when the truth was we were shocked rigid. I had no idea what to say or do. Oblivious, the heroin pair made themselves comfortable on my nice pink couch. I thought they'd never go. When they finally did, we raced round to Mandy's flat and banged on the door.

'You'll never believe what's just happened!'

Although I'd taken stuff now and then, drugs really weren't my thing and heroin was never ever on my radar. It was a frightening, ugly drug. Some of the lads I knew from the ice rink ended up on it and overdosed. The couple who brought it into my flat that day are both dead now.

In 1986, I started a course in English and Drama at Childwall College, thinking I'd get a teaching qualification. It was the actress Glenda Jackson who'd put the idea into my head. When she was in Liverpool filming *Business As Usual* with Cathy Tyson, I got wind she was at the Adelphi and raced across town to see her. I spotted her coming out of the hotel and chased after her up the road. I said I was an aspiring actress and would be glad of any advice she had for me. She told me to make sure I had another skill to fall back on if things didn't work out, so I went to college. I found it tough, studying, doing bar work in the evenings, plays at weekends, looking after Dannielle. There weren't enough hours in the day and trying to get assignments done was a nightmare. I couldn't cope, and after a year I dropped out.

Every year I had a party for Dannielle's birthday. When she was five the bash was at the Holiday Inn and I booked fire-eaters and stilt-walkers, people I'd met through the Rathbone. I sat up all night wrapping ridiculous amounts of presents for her, completely over the top, determined to give her the world. I kept all her birthday cards, filed them away in order. I still have them. She always had a birthday cake and candles, which was something I'd never had, and it niggled me. A few years ago I had a go at my mother about it and she was incredulous.

'You're upset you never had a cake?' she said. 'We took you all over the world, we gave you everything, and you're complaining you didn't get a cake on your birthday!'

If I was skint, down to the last fiver in my pocket, I'd take Dannielle to the Tate or the William Brown Museum, where you didn't have to pay to go in. Liverpool is the most amazing city architecturally, full of classic buildings, and we'd walk through town, down Duke Street, along Lime Street, and on the way home I'd buy a bag of chips for us to share and we'd sing daft songs and have a ball. Whether I had money or didn't, it made no difference to us. We were happy.

In 1987, the BBC was about to go into production on a new peak-time drama series called *Truckers*, set in St Helen's. James Hazeldean was the lead and they were looking for a fat girl for one of the parts. Dorothy Andrew, the casting director who'd seen me play the genie in the production of *Arabian Nights* at the Unity Theatre, reckoned I'd be perfect. If I tell you the nickname of the *Truckers* girl was 'the St Helen's Butter Mountain' you'll get an idea of just how big I was. I got called for an audition at Mersey Television. This was years before I got my part in *Brookside*, and I was dead excited. So much was resting on it. If all went well, everything would change for the better. I got recalled to the BBC in London to see the producer, Terry Williams, and one of the directors, Jeremy Summer.

I got the part. I. GOT. THE. PART!

It was phenomenal, everything I'd dreamed of. I'd landed a TV role and a twelve-month contract with the *fucking BBC*! I signed up and the scripts came through and I was absolutely ecstatic. This was it, the break I had dreamed of. A few days before we were due to start filming, one of the directors phoned.

'Just checking, but you have got an Equity card, haven't you?'

I hadn't. It had never crossed my mind I needed one. No one had said a word about it. Until then. I explained I'd been training and had only done a few things. On the other end of the phone there was a second or two of silence and then he said, 'Oh my God.'

Not good, then. 'You're joking,' he went on. 'You really don't have an Equity card?'

No joke, I really didn't. From his reaction, it was obviously a massive deal.

For the next few hours the phone calls went back and forth, via London and Manchester, while they tried to sort things out. I was in a terrible state, worried and worked up and horribly stressed. Those few hours were horrendous. I went round to me mum's and lay on the couch, sobbing. My dad turned up. I'd been told to expect a call by five o'clock at the latest to tell me one way or another. The hours dragged. At five sharp the phone rang. They were very sorry but without an Equity card they couldn't proceed.

That was it. I'd lost the job. I was distraught, inconsolable, absolutely broken-hearted. Nothing my parents could say or do helped. Over the next few hours I became hysterical, deranged. That night, 6 March, the Zeebrugge ferry, *The Herald of Free Enterprise*, went down, and my dad was watching the news, saying how terrible it was. I was in such a state I wasn't taking it in, not one bit, and ended up screaming at him, going, 'I don't give a shit!' It was impossible to calm me down, and in the end my mum had to get the doctor out to sedate me.

The producer wrote to say how sorry he was it hadn't worked out for me. I also got a lovely letter from the director I'd met, Jeremy Summer, sympathizing and wishing me luck. Funny, we ended up working together a few years later at *Brookside*. It took me ages to get over the disappointment. It was a major series, massive, weeks of filming, high-profile work. Dorothy Andrew, God love her, got me in the following week for lunch. She had a reputation at Mersey TV for being proper tough, but she knew how much it had meant to me and she was lovely, so kind.

'I'm so sorry,' she said. 'I will get something else for you.'

It took a few years, but she was true to her word.

This is my mum, Olwyn Evans as she was then (on the left), with her sister, my Aunty Doreen, in 1941. Mum would have been around two and Doreen three years old in this picture.

A rare photo of my mum and dad, Frank and Olwyn, together on one of their many foreign holidays. This is in Italy, in 1968.

My parents didn't take many photos of me when I was a little girl, so these pictures of me on various holidays are very precious. Top: In Wales, aged around three in 1966; Middle: me and Mum in Jersey, 1967; Bottom, me (on the left) and a friend in Tangiers, Morocco, 1969.

My brother, Simon, was born in 1970 when I was eight. I adored him and took him everywhere with me.

Simon and our cat, Foss, in our house in Percy Street in 1978.

My daughter Dannielle, aged four months, with my mum at the house in Percy Street in early 1982.

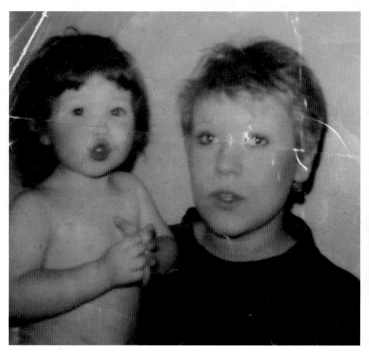

Me (looking very thin!) and Danielle, aged around eighteen months.

Butter wouldn't melt! Dannielle's kindergarten class photo, aged three in 1984. She attended the McKee School of Dance and Drama until she was eleven years old.

Me and Dannielle
in 1983.

Dannielle, aged ten, in
the living room of our
flat in Huskisson Street –
just across the road from
the house I'd grown up
in on Percy Street. We
lived there very happily
for seven years.

To my beautiful Mother
I love you loads
+ loads from
your daughter
xxx

I was made up to join the cast of *Brookside* in 1993, playing Mo McGee. This was my official publicity photo, which I gave as a gift to my mum.

Tina Malone

Out on the town with (L–R) my cousin Carol, my aunt Astrid, my cousin Angela, my mum and, with me in the front, my good friend and *Brookie* castmate Rachael Lindsay.

Me and my beloved dad, Frank in 1990.

Me and Sir John Mills at the Liverpool Empire in 1995. For many years this was the only photo of me that my dad had up on his wall – he liked it because I was with a 'proper actor'.

11

Getting to auditions cost money. I had to pay babysitters, pay for taxis, train fares. I was often broke. My dad was the one who bailed me out. I know he was worried, but even when I was scraping by, earning next to nothing, I never had the slightest doubt I'd make it. No question about it, not in my mind. I was going to do theatre, films, television, everything. For inspiration, I'd sit and read *Songs My Mother Taught Me* by Marlon Brando, *The Moon's a Balloon* by David Niven and *Will There Really Be a Morning?* the autobiography of the actress Frances Farmer. I would read about Jack Nicholson, struggling, going to auditions with a hole in his shoe, feeling like he was better than the part he was being asked to play. Every story I read, I identified with. I'd think, *That's me – that's how I feel.* Call it arrogant, but I had an unshakeable belief that I was born to be an actor, that whatever talent I had was natural, raw.

I was mixing with people who'd been to the Central School of Speech and Drama, in London, and RADA, and had a bit of a chip on my shoulder that I'd not had the same formal training. I felt I'd missed out, wasn't quite up to the level of some of my contemporaries. When Dannielle was about five, I got all the forms for RADA and paid my twenty quid for the audition, but in the end I didn't go through with the application. I kept thinking, what if I get in? What then? I couldn't move to London, not with Dannielle. Even if my dad was willing to support me financially, no way would I even think about going without having my child with me. It didn't matter how I looked at it, RADA was never going to happen, and that was a source of huge disappointment. It was only years later when I met wonderful actors like Kathy Burke and Ray Winstone that I realized there were plenty of outstanding people who hadn't been to RADA and it hadn't made the slightest difference.

Having done two stints at the Rathbone I couldn't go back a third time. That was the rule, no way round it. I missed the people, the buzz, the work, and kept calling in on Peter Ward. I decided to write a play and asked if he would direct it. He turned me down.

'You direct it,' he said. 'You know what you're doing.'

From what I'd seen, most acting jobs went to men, so I decided to write something with an all-female cast, and came up with *A Man for All Reasons*, a story of love and betrayal. I loved the writing process and was inspired by my love of history, the Tudors, and the 1966 film about Sir Thomas More, *A Man For All Seasons*, starring Paul Scofield, who won the Oscar for Best Actor. I stuck a notice on the board at the

Rathbone inviting anyone interested to audition. Quite a few turned up and I cast a bunch of talented women – Michaela, Fran, Lisa, Debbie, Di and Gaynor. Since I was always making cracks, the company ended up being called Wisecrack. The logo, a pair of scarlet lips, was inspired by my trademark red lippy.

I went to the Unity Theatre and spoke to the artistic director, Graeme Phillips, about putting the play on for three nights. I had no money and did a box-office split with them. It was incredible for me to see my name on the billing as writer, producer and director. People were interested in this feisty single mother from Toxteth with her Staffordshire bull terrier and hamsters and her theatre company. We got rave reviews in the *Liverpool Echo* and actors like Paul McGann and John McArdle came to see us. The Unity was only a small theatre, 120 seats, but it was sold out. I'll never forget peering into the audience from the wings and seeing famous people off the telly who had paid to see my little play. I was gobsmacked. The *Brookside* writer, Jimmy McGovern, was there as well.

Seeing my work performed was exciting and at the same time nerve-racking – much worse than actually being on stage, because once the curtain goes up it's out of your hands. We made about £400, which was phenomenal, and the theatre suggested doing it again. Graeme Phillips became massively significant in my life, kind and supportive, full of encouragement. He also let me do the box office in between plays to earn a bit of extra money.

In 1989 I wrote another play, *Lipstick, Rations and Rouge*, set during the Second World War and timed to coincide with the fiftieth anniversary of the outbreak of the conflict. It was commissioned by Liverpool City Libraries and had £5,000 of funding from the Independent Theatre Council, which was a massive deal and meant I was able to pay me and the girls the Equity minimum of £209 a week for the six weeks we toured, mainly playing to audiences of pensioners who had lived through the war. We also got our Equity cards.

As Wisecrack went from strength to strength, I wrote another play, *What Do You Mean, 1992?*, about the European Union and the creation of the euro and what it meant for us in the UK. The play was a journey through Europe, looking at the other countries in the EU and our connection with them, and was very funny. I got a lot of input from the other girls, Fran and Lisa in particular, and Gaynor, who came up with funny lines. We became close, really good friends, and I loved the discipline of the work, writing, and getting together to rehearse at my flat in Huskisson Street. I approached an actress called Noreen Kershaw to direct *1992*. I'd seen Noreen in the stage version of Willy Russell's *Shirley Valentine* at the Everyman and she had blown me away. The play transferred to the Festival of Comedies at the Liverpool Playhouse and sold out.

Around the same time, I got Jim Hitchmough, the writer of the TV comedy series *Watching*, on board. He was from Liverpool and had seen my first play, *A Man For All Reasons*, and sent me a lovely encouraging letter and a cheque for £100. We became great friends and he and I wrote the next play, *Waiting For H (And Then There Were Five)*, about the six wives of Henry VIII. I got Arts Council funding and, again, Noreen Kershaw directed. From being a little girl I'd been obsessed with Anne Boleyn, ever since I'd seen Geneviève Bujold in the role opposite Richard Burton in the film *Anne of the Thousand Days*. We needed a poster to promote the play and Noreen suggested using an old church on Rodney Street as a backdrop.

The Church of St Andrew was derelict and we had to climb over railings in our costumes to get in. The church was famous for its pyramid-shaped tomb of an entrepreneur, William Mackenzie. As I posed beside the tomb, I thought nothing of it. It was only much later I came across the story of Mackenzie, known in Liverpool as the Rodney Street ghost. Rodney Street was very close to where we had lived in Percy Street and when I finally unearthed a picture of Mackenzie at the William Brown Street Library, I knew him straight away. He was the man in the cloak and top hat who kept showing up in my bedroom when I was a child. There was no doubt in my mind. I was euphoric. Whatever anyone else had thought at the time, I knew I had not been imagining things. My parents had never believed I was seeing a ghost when I was little, so when, all those years on, I was able to tell them the story and finally get them to acknowledge that what I'd gone through was real and not something inside my head, it gave me a sense of peace.

The last production Wisecrack did was *Sex, Pies and Sellotape*, a comedy about a gang of girls in a flat all trying to get a date, which I wrote and co-directed with Noreen. As Wisecrack got more established I got more and more attention and did loads of press and radio interviews. Radio 4's arts programme, *Kaleidoscope*, gave me a Woman of the Year award in 1990. I'd set out to create work for women in an industry where it was hard to come by, and to get all of us an Equity card, which I'd done. It seemed the right time to wind up the company.

I was up and down to London auditioning for everything from *The Bill* and *Holby* to adverts for Utterly Butterly, getting bits of work, earning a few quid here and there, not enough to cover the cost of the audition most of the time. A sixty-quid fee was never going to change the world. Dannielle was doing bits of modelling and acting and there were always classes and auditions for her to get to as well. She'd got a small part in the film *The Dressmaker* in 1988, with Joan Plowright and Jane Horrocks, who was fresh out of RADA, and that was the first time I'd been on a film set. I was in awe of Joan Plowright, who was big and bustling and had real presence. I used to watch her, thinking, 'That's Olivier's wife!' Crazy times. I worked like mad and made myself available for parts – pushed and pushed. I pawned, borrowed, bummed and begged to get to auditions, and my mum and dad subsidized me through it all.

When Dannielle was about eight, my mum started seeing a man called Ghassan Ossman, who was training to be a doctor. Mum was fifty then and Ghassan was about twenty years younger. My father never actually met him but thoroughly disapproved on principle. He was still hoping to patch things up with Mum. Ghassan was from Syria; a lovely, kind man. He adored my mother and they seemed happy. He wasn't much older than me and we got on, had huge heated debates about the Lebanon and Palestine, which we really enjoyed but left my mother bored out of her head.

They'd been together a couple of years when they got married in 1991. My dad was appalled on every level, convinced Ghassan was after her money, eyeing up her pension – not that there was anything to suggest his feelings weren't genuine. Mum seemed happy enough and that was all that mattered. When Ghassan got a job in Malaysia, Mum stayed in Liverpool and went out to see him every three months. I think she quite liked the fact they only saw each other for a few weeks here and there, and, inevitably, they drifted apart. After they'd been married about five years, he moved back to Syria and that proved the final nail in the coffin of their relationship. Mum asked him to collect his things and they got divorced. It was all very amicable.

Of course, my dad was delighted.

Both my parents were supportive of my acting and came to see everything I did, although I don't think my dad took me too seriously in the early days. He was always asking when I was going to get a proper job. He loved the social side of what I was doing, coming down to the Everyman Bistro and mixing with my friends, who were either quirky or gay or transsexual. My mum just loved coming to see me on stage and having a night out at the theatre. She did the majority of babysitting and my dad did the majority of baling me out financially. I couldn't have done it without their support. I think more than anything they saw my tenacity, and after a while my dad realized I wasn't about to pack it in.

In 1991, things started looking up. Frank Clarke, who'd written *Letter to Brezhnev*, was casting his next film, *Blonde Fist*, and had seen me in a play at the Unity, *Now or Never*. He asked around and Lyn Kelly, a friend of mine from the

Rathbone, who knew Frank and his sister, Margi, put him in touch with me. At the time, the Clarkes were absolute legends in Liverpool. Margi had starred in *Brezhnev* with Alfred Molina. It was a huge opportunity for me. I went for the audition, got it, and will be forever grateful to Lyn, who now writes for *Coronation Street* under her married name, Papadopoulos.

Everything was happening at once. A couple of weeks after getting *Blonde Fist*, the director Terence Davies was in town casting for his second film, *The Long Day Closes*. Like Frank Clarke, Terence was also a bit of a god in Liverpool. The year before, his first film, *Distant Voices, Still Lives*, had won the prestigious Palme d'Or in Cannes.

I walked into the Adelphi, the same place I'd auditioned for Frank Clarke, and when I saw who else was there thought I had no chance. Joy Blakeman and Denise Thomas were sitting there. Mark Womack, Paul McGann, Gary Mavers. All the others got a recall and I didn't. I was gutted. Two days later I got a call to say the part of Edna, a big blowsy woman with a fondness for fur coats and red lippy, was mine.

The film was set in the fifties and we spent weeks on location in Rotherhithe in south-east London and Liverpool. I loved it. Dannielle got to play the Virgin Mary in a Nativity scene, although that got cut. Marjorie Yates was the lead. I got close to Scouse actresses Joy Blakeman and Denise Thomas. Denise had been at the Rathbone and then RADA. Joy had also trained at RADA. I still had a bit of an inferiority complex about not having gone down that road but, in all honesty, they were both so beautiful and such brilliant actresses, I was flattered they wanted to be my friend.

Terence Davies was gentle and softly spoken, unassuming. His style of direction was precise and meticulous. Frank Clarke was the opposite, as loud and out there as Terence was quiet and reserved. I loved working with both of them.

In *Blonde Fist*, I played a big fat daft scrubber with peroxide hair, black eyes and a squeaky voice. In *The Long Day Closes*, I was the warm-hearted neighbour with a cheeky-chappy husband played by an old-school Liverpool actor, Jimmy Wilde.

That same year, 1991, I also landed the part of a fairy princess for a VW car advert. It was ridiculous money. I had costume fittings in London and was whisked off to Paris, first class, then on to the Loire Valley for the shoot. All I had to do was sit in a carriage and pull a face that said I was really pissed off. It was twenty seconds on screen, if that. Peter Falk, the TV detective Colombo, did the voiceover. They must have had money to burn.

When I got my first payment through, a cheque for £10,000, I felt as if I'd hit the jackpot. For years I'd been struggling, not earning enough to cover my outgoings a lot of the time, so it was a huge amount of money in one go, and there was more to come. First thing I did was give my dad a couple of grand. He nearly passed out. Having bailed me out for years and never had anything back, it must have been a shock to be on the receiving end. I took my mum shopping to Cavern Walks, to Wade Smith, which had three floors full of designer labels. Mum got some Armani pants and a top and I got a little cotton Tommy Hilfiger dress and some pink Dolce & Gabbana sandals with diamantes. I wore those shoes to death and still have them in their original box. After making do with a clapped-out old washer, my biggest extravagance was a top-of-the-range Hotpoint washing machine and dryer. Once they were plumbed in, I felt like a new woman.

Life was good. I was twenty-eight, working hard, doing well. I was also fat. Since starting at the Rathbone I'd really piled on the weight. When I started acting I was around 10 stone 7 pounds but it was creeping up. I would gain a stone or two, go on some daft fad diet, lose it, and then in the course of the next few months it would all go back on again. I'd got into a destructive cycle of losing a couple of stone and putting three back on, losing two, gaining four. I'd go from a size 12 to an 18, back to a 12. Once the weight started going on, I couldn't seem to get it under control. Over the next ten years I reckon I put on about 6 stone and went up to a size 20.

Around that time a few actresses, ones I'd call big birds, were doing well: Pauline Quirke, Jo Brand, Caroline Quentin, Dawn French. I'd signed with an agent, Shane Collins, and for the first few years I was with him, every job I went for wanted a 'Dawn French/Roseanne Barr type'. I'd go, 'You mean a fat bird?' If they wanted a pretty girl there'd be millions to choose from, but there weren't that many fat ones, so in some respects being big was no bad thing.

My dad used to have a go at me. 'You know why you're fat,' he'd say. 'It's because in your game you can be anything you like and they'll accept you and you've fallen into thinking, "Well, I'll be a fat bastard, then." That's what gives you an excuse to shovel in more food.'

My size was starting to seriously depress me. I was getting

through huge amounts of food. I couldn't eat one packet of crisps, I had to have the whole pack of six. I didn't want one bar of chocolate, I wanted eight. Two drinks were never enough, I wanted twenty. Everything in my life was to excess. I'd be with someone for six months and have sex every day three times a day. Even when it came to work, I didn't want to rehearse for two or three hours like everyone else. I'd be going, 'Why can't we rehearse all day? Why can't we do ten hours?'

My mood swings were terrible.

In my early twenties I'd been diagnosed with diabetes. What started with me going to the doctor to complain about horrendous periods ended with an overnight stay in the Royal Liverpool Hospital being tested for fibroids and polycystic ovaries, among other things. They weighed and measured me, checked my urine, and diagnosed type 2 diabetes. From then on I was injecting insulin three times a day.

'It's because you're fat,' was my dad's reaction.

Having diabetes never curbed my eating or drinking. If anything, it made me worse because the insulin stabilized me and gave me a sense of well-being, which was definitely not what the doctors intended.

Blonde Fist had its premiere at the Edinburgh Film Festival in 1991. I went with my friend from the Rathbone, Lyn Kelly, and we spent the whole weekend drinking, having a good time. My VW advert was all over the telly; I had thousands in the bank and was making my big-screen debut in a Frank Clarke film. I was on a high. Tired and hung over, I came home from Edinburgh loaded down with presents for Dannielle and my mum, walked into my flat in Huskisson Street, and found my dad there with my brother, Simon, and his girlfriend, Sue. They were, like, 'Surprise!' While I'd been away they'd redecorated. In the living room, a lavish curtain in a pink and purple print to match the suite had gone up. It was huge, a complicated silk affair, all swags and tails. My brother had been to Ikea, got some black shelving and put it up in the living room. All my books were in neat rows. The whole place was tidy, uncluttered. It wasn't how I had left it and I was not a bit grateful and started wailing. I was furious, hysterical. It's hard to explain what made me flip. The reasonable side of me could see what they'd done was kind and thoughtful. At the same time, it triggered a sense of overwhelming panic. For a while I had been going through a period of feeling really low, crying all the time, getting horribly upset and not knowing why. I had been to see my GP, Dr Flynn, and told him some of what was going on.

It was obvious something wasn't right.

My meltdown when I got back from Edinburgh was exactly the kind of thing I had tried to explain to my doctor. Everyone had seen me blow a gasket before. I often threw things, whatever came to hand. Luckily, my aim was rubbish. I chucked a portable TV at Simon one day, sent it sailing through the open window and into a flower bed. I hurled a tin of Pedigree Chum at my friend John Hart when we were arguing about something, and it lodged in the kitchen wall, where it stayed for years.

The day they rearranged my flat, nothing got thrown, but I had to take all the books down and put them back the way

I wanted them. I knew my behaviour was irrational but I couldn't help it. I really thought I was off my head, going mad.

Not long after, I was diagnosed with bipolar and obsessive compulsive disorder.

12

What my doctor said about me being bipolar made sense. Not that he called it bipolar. I don't think anyone was using that term in 1991. It was manic depression and it explained a lot about my behaviour, my mood swings and ups and downs. Getting the diagnosis didn't worry me; it actually spurred me on to do a lot of reading and find out as much as I could about my so-called condition. Thankfully, my GP didn't want to throw medication at me. I wouldn't have wanted to take anything. I preferred to manage without drugs if I could. I'm actually happy with what I call my madness, if that makes sense. I like it. It lets me know who I am and gives me a reality check from time to time, helps me get a grip. When things are bad, I look at what other people are going through, in my own city and around the world, and realize I'm doing OK.

I really wanted a part in the Channel 4 soap, *Brookside*, and kept writing to Phil Redmond, owner of Mersey TV and creator of the show, to ask if there was anything going. I'd get a polite 'thanks but nothing doing' back. It didn't put me off. I had my heart set on *Brookie*. Once a few weeks had gone by I'd write again. *Hiya! Just wondered if there might be anything coming up . . . ?* I'd tell him what I'd been doing, how much I loved the show and so on. Poor Phil, it probably drove him mad.

By then, I'd done lots of theatre work, *Blonde Fist, The Long Day Closes,* and the Willy Russell film *Terraces,* with Mark Womack and Paul Broughton, which Rob Rohrer directed for the BBC. It pays to be persistent and, in 1993, I got the part of Mo McGee in *Brookside.* I don't suppose those letters to Phil Redmond had anything to do with it. It was more likely that Dorothy Andrew, the casting director who'd suggested me for *Truckers,* the BBC series that fell through because I didn't have my Equity card a few years earlier, had been keeping me in mind, as she promised she would.

If there was ever anywhere I was going to fit right in it was *Brookside,* or so I thought, but at that time there weren't many actresses around who were also single parents. Most of the women I mixed with were professional and had been to drama school in London so, once again, I was unusual. Too posh for some, too common for others. It seemed to be the story of my life.

After seven good years, I moved out of Huskisson Street when the Liverpool Housing Trust offered me a deal; they said if I could raise a deposit to buy a place, they would match it. I had £8,000, which they made up to £16,000, and I bought a lovely terraced house in Belvoir Road, Widnes.

Dannielle was ready to change schools anyway, and got into Fairfield High, which wasn't far from our new place. Before we moved, I got fined £1,000 for not having a TV licence. It was one of those things that slipped my mind and the detector van nabbed me. Lucky I'd done that VW advert and had a bit of cash.

To me, *Brookside* was the best soap on TV. It was shot on single camera like a drama, which wasn't how the other soaps were done, and was the best training ground in the world. Phil Redmond took on the most diverse mix of people, some fresh from film school, others from the streets, and created something special. People say that soap is formulaic, but *Brookside* never was. It was ground-breaking, and did things the other, more established soaps would never have dreamed of, like Anna Friel's famous lesbian kiss. To me, Phil Redmond was a genius. My only complaint was that I never got to do as much as I'd have liked. A couple of times, I went to see Phil to ask for a bigger storyline. I really felt they could have done a lot more with me and I was never sure why they didn't. I got on well with Phil and Mal Young, the producer, but never felt I was in the A Team. Or the B Team, come to think of it.

I suspected a bit of it was to do with the size I was. I was huge, an 18 or 20, and there weren't any fat birds in the soaps at the time. I remember thinking they were scared because I was big, or maybe they thought I was too inexperienced. That was never going to change unless they took the plunge and gave me more to do. All the same, I was phenomenally grateful, because the series gave me my TV training – taught me how to hit my mark, get out of another actor's light and make sure other actors kept out of my light. It was hard work, a treadmill at times, but wonderful. Some of it was shot on the old Childwall College campus where I'd spent a year doing my course in 1986. They make *Hollyoaks* there now, so when my daughter landed the part of Kelly in 2011 she was treading the same path I once did. I'm probably Dannielle's harshest critic, but I was blown away when I saw her in that role.

While I was in *Brookside*, the writer, Jimmy McGovern, decided Jimmy Corkhill's character needed a dog and came up with Cracker. I thought our dog, Kelly, would be perfect. She was full of character, a great little thing, and we knew her timing was good because she'd had a litter of eight pups on Christmas Day 1987. She auditioned, got the part, and turned out to be a natural performer. Only trouble was, she and I couldn't be on set on the same day. If she caught sight of me, she barked the place down. Cracker was supposed to be a boy so on screen Kelly was a 'he' and people kept writing in saying she was a bitch. It didn't matter. She was a good little actor. She spent three years in the soap and had some good storylines, including a dramatic exit when Sinbad ran her down and Jimmy chucked her in the Mersey.

At *Brookside*, I got friendly with Rachael Lindsay, who played Sammy Rogers. Rachael was ten years younger than me and into her yoga and running, but for some reason we got along and became inseparable. She was kind and beautiful and a great friend. We went out loads together. I'd always loved going out clubbing, knocking back the ale, but now it was VIP parties – the opening of *Cats*, *Blood Brothers*, Paul Smith, the designer, throwing a bash in Nottingham. I would always be, 'Yeah, right, we're up for that! Oasis front-row tickets? Yeah! Where is it – Dublin? I'll go!'

A good friend of ours, an actor, Vinny Davies, was best mates with Paul Gallagher, Liam and Noel's brother, and the four of us were often out together. Vinny always knew a club with a doorman who'd get us in, so we were never stuck for somewhere to go. We started going to Dublin a lot. A dear friend, Dave Egan, had a club called Lillie's Bordello, which was famous. You needed a key to get in. No key, no entry. The VIP room, the Library, was done out like a gentleman's club with big leather armchairs and books lining the walls. Shane MacGowan from the Pogues was a regular, so was Patrick Kielty. Dermot Morgan, of *Father Ted* fame, was often there and so was Ardal O'Hanlon.

We hung out with whoever was in, drinking Bollinger, dancing. Sometimes I was that pissed I didn't know what day it was. I drank so much I would vomit and carry on. A typical night at Lillie's would see us heading back to the Westbury Hotel at six in the morning. We'd crash out, get some sleep, go shopping, and get ready for another night on the town. This could go on for three or four nights. If there was a celebrity in Dublin, they'd find their way to Lillie's. I've been in there with Julian Lennon, and Courtney Cox, from *Friends*, who came in one night with the actor Aidan Quinn.

When Patrick Bergin, who had been in *Sleeping with the Enemy* with Julia Roberts, came in, we got chatting. Patrick Bergin was dark with a big 'tashe.

'I thought you were great in *A Fish Called Wanda*,' Rachael said, mistaking him for Kevin Kline.

Patrick Bergin gave her a withering look. I don't suppose

any film star likes being taken for someone else. 'I wasn't in *A Fish Called Wanda*,' he said.

None the wiser, Rachael gave him a smile. 'I loved that film. You were brilliant.'

Patrick Bergin made his excuses and left.

I fell about laughing.

In those days a typical night out for me would start off with a bottle of champagne at home while I was getting ready, then some spirits. I could put away thirty or forty gin and tonics no trouble, half a bottle of brandy, a bottle of champagne, ten bottles of Beck's. I'd think nothing of piling into a cab and going to another city to keep the party going. Half the time, it was a case of, 'Yay, let's go to Leeds!' Or Manchester. Or wherever. A night out could roll into a five-night bender. I'd end up in some states, in a flat somewhere with a load of dodgy people I didn't know. In those days, I could go to a party in Leeds and end up in Glasgow, making a quick exit when a fight kicked off or the guy next to me got a gun out. It was proper frightening at times, doing a runner, ending up on a street in a strange town, thinking, where the fuck am I?

We'd go out for a full English breakfast at a Little Chef then crash out and sleep all day. I wasn't promiscuous and I never hurt anyone, so I felt entitled to go out and have fun when I wasn't working. When it came to *Brookside* I was serious. I learnt my lines and showed up on time, always.

I was dabbling with bits and bobs of drugs, nothing heavy. I was never that bothered about drugs, but if they were on offer I'd have them. Basically, I could take them or leave them. Whether it was a spliff, a tablet, a line of coke or whatever, my drug of choice was always going to be alcohol.

I knew I was drinking way too much. I'd say, 'I've got to stop.' I'd do four days on *Brookside*, no booze, and think I was doing good. As long as the drink wasn't affecting work it was a case of, 'I've done a big storyline, I knew every line and never messed up, so that's all right, then.' I kidded myself I was managing it. Any worries I had about how much drink I was getting through went into a box and got filed away. It was my way of coping. Put the difficult stuff in a compartment and forget about it. I'm still like that.

I couldn't do it with my weight, though.

In the space of a few years I'd put on almost 6 stone. My eating was out of control. I was always on some diet: cabbage soup, grapefruit, food combining, low fat, no fat, Cambridge, Lighter Life. I found out everything there was to know about nutrition. For months on end I'd go to the gym, five days a week. I tried Weight Watchers, Slimming World. I knew what I had to do and the diets worked, up to a point. I couldn't stick to them long term, that was the problem. I'd lose weight and in no time I'd be stuffing my face again and it would all go back on, plus a bit more. The more I yo-yo dieted, the bigger I got. It was horrible, depressing. I was starting to hate myself. I knew my OCD and bipolar disorder made me prone to overeating.

I was the kind of person who couldn't moderate. With me, it was all or nothing. If I stayed in, we'd sit in front of the telly watching garbage and eating chippy food. Chinese takeaways. Sweets, chocolate. Any old rubbish. Then it was back on the booze and no proper food for three or four days at a time. I was in *Brookside*, doing personal appearances, getting £1,500 to open a nightclub, having a ball. I went from one extreme to another – highs and lows, ups and downs, euphoric partying and crushing, crippling depression. After three or four days of drinking in Dublin, my feet would swell so badly my ankles were like balloons and I wouldn't be able to get my shoes on to board the plane to go home. I'd get back to Widnes, worse for wear, loaded down with presents for Dannielle, like a scene from the drama *Ab Fab*, teetering in stinking of gin, Dannielle in her school uniform at the table doing her homework, telling me I was disgusting.

While I was away, my mum looked after my daughter, so I always knew she was being cared for, but it can't have been easy for her being an only child with a single parent who was mad as a March hare at times, as well as being famous. It's only recently she has told me how hard it was growing up with her mother in the public eye. In lots of respects, Dannielle had a wonderful life, mixed with interesting people, had all kinds of experiences, and it made her liberal and outspoken and confident. The downside was my profile meant I would draw comments that weren't always favourable – in newspapers and so on, and she found that hard to deal with. While I was out partying, I still had a mortgage and bills to pay and I was neglecting them, being stupid and irresponsible and spending beyond my means, living the high life. It couldn't carry on.

In 1995, rehearsing for panto, I got a wake-up call.

13

I was playing Baroness Hardup in *Cinderella* at the Regent Theatre in Hanley, Stoke-on-Trent, staying at the Holiday Inn. Dannielle was at home in Widnes with my mum.

I'd been in rehearsals for twenty-four hours, everything going well, getting on with Wendy Turner, Tristan Bancks and the rest of the cast, looking forward to the next couple of weeks. We finished work and I had a few drinks with the others in the hotel bar. I didn't go mad, not by my standards, five or six gin and tonics and that was it, before I called it a night. Once I was in my room on my own, I started to have a panic attack. It came out of nowhere and I couldn't get my breath. My heart was racing, I felt dreadful, ready to collapse. I rang reception and asked them to call a doctor. Someone came up to check on me, found me on the floor and dialled 999. The paramedics arrived, gave me oxygen and got me on a stretcher. As they wheeled me out into the corridor, the door of the room opposite opened and the director, Jeffrey Longmore, watched open-mouthed as I went past, doing my best to give him a reassuring smile from under the oxygen mask.

At the City General Hospital they put me on a saline drip and ran blood tests. I was dehydrated and had acute hypertension. My diabetes was out of control. Once they stabilized me, the doctor grilled me on my smoking and drinking habits.

I told him I was on forty cigs a day, that I only drank on a Thursday, Friday and Saturday. Sunday, sometimes.

'How much do you drink on an average night out?'

'Thirty or forty G&Ts, brandy, champagne. If I'm on the beer it's ten bottles of Beck's or Bud.'

He looked at me. 'Right. You're an alcoholic.'

I was staggered. 'I can't be. It's not like I drink every day.'

My idea of an alcoholic was an unkempt bloke on a park bench with a can of Special Brew. That wasn't me. When I said as much, he laughed, told me I was being ridiculous.

'Don't be so naive. You've come in stinking of alcohol. You drink too much, you smoke too much. You eat too much. You're morbidly obese. Your blood sugars are all over. Frankly, the state of your liver, it should be in a bed of its own.'

I didn't want to believe it, especially not the bit about being an alcoholic. 'I'm a social drinker,' I said.

'You're an alcoholic. Carry on the way you are and with your blood pressure, anxiety, diabetes and everything else going on, you'll be dead in two years.'

I was absolutely terrified.

I'd gone to Stoke-on-Trent thinking life was great. I had my own home, money coming in, I was dating, messing about with different blokes, having a laugh, but oh my God, I was eating too much, drinking too much, smoking too much, partying too much. No wonder I was ill. All those chippy meals, Chinese takeaways, pasties, sweets, chocolates, gin and tonics, brandies, beer, champagne. I lay in bed thinking about what the doctor had said. OK, I had overdone things, but I was *not* an alcoholic. The way I saw it was that alcoholics drank vodka because you couldn't smell it, so the fact I'd never touched the stuff meant I couldn't be one.

The next day I was back at the theatre and straight back on the drink.

On opening night two days later I was in the wings drinking port and brandy from a mug before I went on. No one knew. My body had got so used to alcohol I could get through vast quantities without getting drunk. Every night I went on stage and did a great job. 'Tina Malone delivers her lines with wicked throwaway technique,' the *Stage* said. I put all the scary stuff the doctor had said into one of my boxes and filed it away out of sight. All over Christmas I was on the shots, sambuca and tequila. I loved me tequila. Mrs Party. I got wrecked. The £2,000 I was getting paid each week went on my bar bill.

I told myself it was fine to get blitzed because it was my last bender. I would stop drinking on New Year's Eve.

When it came to publicity for *Brookside*, there was a pecking order. The highest-profile actors were the likes of Sue Johnston, Ricky Tomlinson, John McArdle, Dean Sullivan,

Sue Jenkins, Steven Pinder and Paul Usher. They played Sheila and Bobby Grant, Billy Corkhill, Jimmy Corkhill, Jackie Corkhill, Max Farnham and Barry Grant, and were household names.

Then you had the younger cast members like Anna Friel (Beth Jordache), Diane Burke (Katy Rogers), Alex Fletcher (Jackie Dixon). There were some older, attractive women too: Mary Tamm (Penny Crosbie), Gabby Glaister (Patricia Farnham), Karen Drury (Susannah Farnham).

Then there was me, the big fat one.

I didn't get asked to do as much as the others – the odd photo shoot for fat bird catalogues, which I hated – so, on the rare occasion I got asked to do something interesting, I jumped at it.

At that time, in the late nineties, Channel 4's *Big Breakfast* show with Chris Evans and Gaby Roslin was huge. When I got invited on to do a sketch with the puppets, Zig and Zag, I was made up. We played a silly game called Tina's Arena where I came up with my top actors of all time, my favourite men, all that kind of daft stuff. It was right up my street. I'm a sucker for a list, always have been. With my Top Ten men they did a kind of chart rundown set to music. I had huge stars like Al Pacino, Robert De Niro, Sean Penn, Robert Carlyle and Ray Winstone, but in the Number One slot was the Scouse actor Jimmy Mulville. No one could believe it. *Jimmy Mulville – he's a ginger!* I was laughing my head off and at the same time deadly serious. He *was* my Number One man. Funny, clever, cute – and a Scouser. His company, Hat Trick Productions, is behind TV shows like *Outnumbered* and *Have I Got News For You*. I thought he was a genius.

Someone must have seen the item and told him, because he got in touch and we met up and became good friends. If I was in London I'd go and see him at his office in Livonia Street and we'd have a cup of tea and a catch-up.

I was trying and failing to stop drinking. I would come off the ale and stay sober for a few days, a week or two if I was lucky, then be back on it as bad as ever. Even after what had happened in Stoke and the stark reality of being told I was killing myself, I still couldn't stop. My liver was a mess, my pancreas was fucked, and I was scared to death. Being fat and not being able to do anything about my weight was making me suicidal. On top of everything, financially, I was all over the place.

Jimmy Mulville saved my life.

I would look at him and think he had everything sorted. I looked up to him. The last thing I wanted was for him to find out what an almighty mess I was, so whenever I saw him I pretended everything was fine and, on the surface, it was. I had work, money coming in, a nice home. It was only half the story. When Jimmy encouraged me to get a showreel together, I didn't want to admit I hadn't the money to do it. I went out of my way to keep what was really going on in my life well hidden.

One day, in his office, I broke down and all the stuff I'd been burying came pouring out – how I wanted to kill myself because I was fat, that I was broke, drinking myself to death.

Jimmy Mulville had been there. He had fought his own demons. His battles with drink and drugs have been well documented. He knew exactly what I was going through.

'You're an alcoholic,' he said, echoing the doctor in Stoke-on-Trent.

I was still having trouble facing it. 'I don't drink every day,' I said. 'I can stop, not have a drink for a week.' It sounded feeble, even to me.

'If you think like that, you've got a problem,' he said.

Jimmy helped me out financially, paid off some of my debts. He encouraged me to go to Alcoholics Anonymous meetings in London and Liverpool. I don't think I'd have got there without him. The idea of being in a room filled with strangers and owning up to the extent of my drink problem frightened the life out of me. I used to sit, feeling the panic rise in my chest, and it was months before I found the courage to stand up and say anything.

It was the first step to getting sober.

14

I'd been in *Brookside* a few years and loved it. Being in a soap had raised my profile and I'd got used to being in the papers and people coming up to me in the supermarket or whatever. It went with the territory.

One day I was at home in Widnes with Rachael and my mum when there was a knock on the door. It was the woman from the local shop to say some fella had been asking about me and Dannielle, wanting to know where we lived. He had photos, of me, and of Dannielle in her school uniform. It all seemed very odd. My mother immediately wanted to know who I owed money to, but I couldn't think of anyone. No one who'd go round showing people photos of me and Dannielle, at any rate. For the next few days it preyed on my mind. I hadn't a clue what it was about.

A week or so later, I got a call from Dannielle's dad. I'd not heard from Jimmy in years. From the day I told him I was pregnant, he hadn't wanted to know. Before that, even. The last time I'd seen him, when I'd taken Dannielle to visit her grandparents, he'd slammed the door in my face and told them not to let me in. Not what you'd call on good terms. As soon as I heard his voice, I was suspicious.

'What do you want?' I said.

He started going on about when we'd first met and him going to prison. All sorts of stuff going back years. I was gobsmacked.

'So, I was only with you a few weeks and the first two nights we were together we never had sex, did we?' he said. 'And do you remember when you said to me . . . ?' All this, out of nowhere. It was absolutely bizarre. I wanted to know what was going on, why he was bringing all this stuff up – and why was he talking in such a weird fucking way?

'What's going on? Why are you asking about all this?'

'Oh, I'm thinking of getting a DNA test done over Dannielle . . . '

I went ballistic. 'She's sixteen years old. What, you think you can come into her life all of a sudden? You can fuck off!'

'No, I'm just trying to make things clear, that's all.'

It wasn't so much what he was saying as the way he was saying it that wasn't right – as if he had someone with him and the conversation was as much for their benefit as mine. I put the phone down. A minute later it rang again. I didn't answer. It rang again.

'Why don't you fuck off and leave me alone?' I said before hanging up.

A minute later it was ringing again. Jimmy said, 'Can I speak to Dannielle?'

I lost it. 'No, you can*not*! Now *fuck off*!'

Over the next few days, Jimmy called again a few times. I had a bad feeling. Something really fucking odd was going on and it was freaking me out. My stress levels were on the ceiling.

The following Saturday, I was at home with Rachael, my mate Vinny, my mum and dad, all of us watching *Blind Date*. The phone went and some guy went, 'Is that Tina Malone? This is so-and-so from the *News of the World*. We're running a story tomorrow about James Cullen, saying he's not the father of your child and that you've tried to get money off him for years.'

I was hysterical. I got on the phone to Jimmy's parents. They were as much in the dark as I was. All night I stayed up waiting for the paper, sick with worry. I had good reason to be. 'Soap's Mo chased me for money over baby for 16 years'. That was what the headline said. The story was splashed across the best part of a full page with pictures. Dannielle was in bits. There it was in black and white, her father saying she wasn't his, that he'd never slept with me. It was all, 'I've never had proper sex with her, there's no way I'm the father but Tina can't get it into her head. It's an obsession.' It devastated Dannielle.

The whole thing was horrendous. I could not believe a newspaper would send a photographer to follow a young girl and snatch pictures of her in her school uniform. How dare they? I was right about those weird calls from Jimmy as well. There had been someone with him – a reporter from the newspaper who was taping them. It stank. I was so upset for my parents and mortified about Dannielle having to go to school and face people after being splashed all over one of the tabloids I got ill and ended up in the Royal Liverpool Hospital with hyper-anxiety for a week. Jimmy's family, appalled by what he'd done, closed ranks around me and Dannielle.

It's bad enough when you're in the public eye having stories sold on you to the papers, believe you me, but when it's your kid getting the flak it's about a million times worse. I went to the Press Complaints Commission and the newspaper was told to print an apology. True to form, the few lines they ran were so well buried on an inside page you had to search to find them.

Since Jimmy was so keen on a DNA test, we had one done, and it confirmed, of course, that Dannielle was his. He was back on the phone full of apologies, saying he'd only sold the story because I was on the telly and doing well. He begged to speak to Dannielle who, understandably, wanted nothing to do with him.

A few weeks later, I gave an interview to the *Mirror*, putting my side of the story, payback for what Jimmy had done, or so I thought. It never crossed my mind it would make things worse. I might as well have lit a fire and chucked petrol on it. Up until then, not even my closest friends or the people I was working with had any idea what had gone on when I was pregnant. I had never spoken about it, had never felt the need. It was something that had been left firmly in the past. Until I raked it up. Dannielle hadn't a clue about me being in a mother and baby home when I was expecting her. Having grown up with the most wonderful relationship with her grandad, she found out he had wanted her adopted and had sent me away when I wouldn't go through with it. She was distraught. Everything she thought she knew no longer held true. I felt as if I'd made things a hundred times worse.

It was a while before we put all that behind us.

15

I was never the type to drink to take the edge off or because I needed Dutch courage. I drank because I loved it. I smoked because I loved it. I dabbled with recreational drugs because I wanted to, not because I felt any peer pressure. What I'm saying is, when it came to my excesses, I only had myself to blame.

It probably took me a couple of years to stop drinking. I'd give up the ale for a week or two, a month, six weeks, and before I knew it, I'd be back on it, as bad as ever. The worst thing I did was try to keep away from everything I associated with alcohol. I'd lock myself in the house for a couple of weeks, thinking I'd steer clear of temptation, but it didn't work. As soon as I was back out in the world again, I'd be straight off the wagon. I found I couldn't stop the going out, the getting wasted, the self-destructive behaviour. Emotionally, I was all over the place. There was a part of me that knew I was funny and good company and talented. I was confident in my ability as an actor. I'd proved it. At the same time, I was horribly insecure because I felt ugly and unloved, a failure. I felt I'd let my parents down. *You drink too much, you smoke too much, you eat too much,* went round and round inside my head.

I wasn't enjoying the drink any more. It wasn't fun. I was a mess. My feet were swollen, I was red-faced, bloated. There was a permanent acrid taste in my mouth. When I went to bed the room would lurch and spin and I'd lie there, hanging on to the mattress, feeling wrecked and sick and full of anxiety. I felt old and ugly, dirty. Over the years, I'd got used to telling myself I didn't mind the after-effects of a bender because I was having a good time. I'd learnt to live like a big, fat, hard-drinking bastard. Now, I was sick of it. I couldn't cope any more with how it made me feel. I'd had a serious wake-up call in Stoke-on-Trent in 1995. Jimmy Mulville had forced me to face facts: *You're an alcoholic.* It was up to me now.

On 30 January 1998, for my thirty-fifth birthday I was in Dublin, staying at the Westbury Hotel, getting ready to party hard with Rachael. I was wearing a black silk shirt and leggings. I'd gone that fat, leggings were all I ever wore. I put on the same blue jacket I always wore, one of those swing styles, massive. I had my hair dark, curly. I looked in the mirror. Jesus Christ, I looked like Demis Roussos.

Rachael, beaming, came along the hotel corridor with a little cake for me. Happy birthday! We were going out, to Lillie's. We'd cracked open the champagne already. I was smiling but inside I felt like shit. I didn't say anything to

Rachael, didn't want to argue. We'd been arguing loads lately. I told myself that once I was out, throwing back the drinks, I'd be fine. We cut the little cake, my head full of *You big ugly fat bastard*, went to Lillie's, and spent the night in the VIP room. Vinny was there. Paul Gallagher had come over from Manchester. There were loads of people, all there to celebrate my birthday. I drank Bollinger all night, but even the champagne couldn't stop the feeling of being weary and nauseated taking hold. I was utterly depressed, sick of the drinking, sick of feeling like crap the next day.

I'd had enough.

A week or so later, Rachael and I were out with Vinny and Noel Gallagher to see an indie band, Smaller, play at the Flying Picket in Liverpool. Noel was big mates with the lead singer, Peter 'Digsy' Deary. Digsy, a Scouser, had inspired Digsy's Diner, one of the tracks on the Oasis *Definitely Maybe* album.

After the gig, me, Rachael, Noel and Vinny ended up in the V&A hotel in Manchester. I was on the gin and tonics, well into double figures, as usual, debating politics with Noel, the pair of us putting the world to rights. Noel kept calling me and Rachael 'Hinge and Bracket'. Rachael was baffled – she had no idea who they were. 'They're men dressed as women – two old spinsters!' I said. We were all pissed, having a laugh. I think it was my idea to play true, dare, kiss, command, promise or tell. I dared Noel to hang Rachael out of the window by her ankles and he nearly did. We were four floors up and he had her halfway out the window before we dragged her back in. I was so drunk I thought it was hysterical. The next day I smelt like a bottle of Gordon's gin. I felt dreadful, so ill I could barely string a sentence together.

On 14 February 1998, Rachael and I were back at the V&A. We met up with Scott Williams, an actor we knew, and a few other friends. I was on the gin and tonic again, feeling greasy and enormous, a complete fucking mess. Drinking wasn't making me happy any more. It hadn't for the last couple of years. It was time to stop.

'This is the last drink I'll have,' I said.

I'm not sure anyone believed me and, with my track record, I couldn't really blame them. I meant it, though.

I've been sober ever since. Once I stopped, that was it. I went to AA meetings on and off and found them helpful, but in all honesty I never felt tempted to touch another drop. As with everything in my life, it had to be a case of all or nothing, and my days of drinking were well and truly over.

In November 1998, I started a ten-month run at the National Theatre in London in *Guiding Star*, a play by the Liverpool writer Jonathan Harvey, directed by Gemma Bodinetz. The backdrop to the story was Hillsborough, where ninety-six people lost their lives on 15 April 1989. The play explored loss, death and survivor guilt – as well as the possibility of recovering in the wake of such a terrible tragedy. I played Marni Sweet, an obese woman whose child was dying from cystic fibrosis as her marriage fell apart. It was a wonderful role, the best part I'd had, lots of big speeches, a real turning point. And it was the National, where every actor wants to go. It was exhilarating, terrifying – like being on a high wire with no safety net.

Every night in the wings, I had an attack of stage fright. My throat was dry, I had sweaty palms, my lip would tremble, my leg would go . . . I called it my Elvis shake. I was never able to relax in my dressing room and wait for my five-minute call. I had to be at the side of the stage, ready, ten minutes before curtain up. In the wings opposite, Kieran O'Brien and Carl Rice, two wonderful young actors, had a habit of peering through a crack in the curtain to see who was in the audience and calling across to me if there were any famous faces. There was always someone: the director Stephen Daldry, the actor Neil Pearson, Janet Street-Porter. Kieran and Carl would be going, 'Tina, look who's in tonight,' and I'd be telling them to shut the fuck up. I couldn't bear anyone talking to me or coming anywhere near me in those few minutes before I went on. I needed to be left alone with my thoughts.

As with most of the theatre work I've done, I was first on. I would take a breath, make the sign of the cross three times and bless myself. The moment I stepped on to the stage and faced the audience the nerves went. The play was well received. Michael Coveney in the *Mail* called it 'one of the best new plays of the year'. I got some good reviews too.

The *Mail on Sunday* said, 'Tina Malone impresses as fat, chain-smoking Marni, a human puff-ball.' In the *Independent*, I was, 'The wonderful Tina Malone as a mountainous, fag-puffing mix of puncturing mordancy and kindly perceptiveness.'

I had some great times in London but I wasn't good at

being away from home. I didn't cope well at all. When I could, I stayed with friends. Jonathan Harvey put me up and so did Kathy Burke. Both were really good to me.

Kathy and I had met years earlier. A lot of the roles I went for, I found myself up against her and another great actress, Annabelle Apsion. Usually, one of them got the part. In 1993, both Kathy and I were up for *Mr Wroe's Virgins*, a series for the BBC directed by Danny Boyle. I got two recalls but didn't get it and was devastated. Kathy got the part of Martha and was mind-blowing in it. At one of the many auditions I went to in London, Kathy and I ended up outside having a fag and got chatting. For years, we were mates. She came to stay with me in Widnes, and if I had an audition in London I'd stay with her in Islington. I'd turn up, sometimes late at night, stressed out, and she would be cooking something amazing, running a bath for me. Without fail, she encouraged me and made me feel supported. When she did *Nil By Mouth* in 1992 with Gary Oldman and Ray Winstone, she invited me on set.

It was Kathy who got me an audition for *Harry Enfield and Chums*, and I played opposite Paul Whitehouse in some new sketches about an Italian couple. In the mid-nineties, Harry, Paul and Kathy were stars, at the top of their game. The show was recorded at the BBC Television Centre in White City, London, in front of an audience. I was terrified and didn't feel I'd done a good job. In the end, a lot of the sketches, including the ones I was in, got dropped. I can't say I was sorry.

Seeing my name in lights at the National was wonderful but at the same time I desperately wanted to be back in

Widnes. I'd always been a home bird and being in London depressed me. Dannielle was seventeen and growing up and I missed her dreadfully. She was pulling away from me and it frightened me. Every week, without fail, I went home. I'd get the train back to Runcorn on a Sunday, a journey that sometimes took seven or eight hours because of some problem or other: faulty signal, points failure, broken-down train on the line ahead . . . I'd lose the whole day, rush about seeing Dannielle and my mum and dad and, on the Monday, be back on the train to London, ready to go on stage the following night.

It got so I hated being in London, absolutely *hated* it.

I would come off stage and be the first one out of the building. Years before, training at the Rathbone, doing plays at the Unity Theatre in Liverpool, earning shit-all, a fiver in my pocket, I'd stay out until the death, until I'd drunk all my money and didn't have enough for a taxi home and had to sleep on someone's couch stinking of booze, because the euphoria of being on stage was so great I couldn't wind down. At the National, I wasn't in the party mood. It was quite a turnaround.

Although I was off the booze, I was messing around with recreational drugs, smoking too much pot – trying to fill the void left by giving up alcohol, maybe, I don't know – and spending too much. I blew a lot of money, not that I could tell you where it went. I'd buy ridiculous things, over-the-top presents, pick up the tab for nights out at the Groucho Club and Soho House. What money I had disappeared. I was coming in late when I had two shows the next day, falling out with people. I was homesick, insecure, a nightmare.

Kathy saw what was happening and tried to talk some sense into me. I didn't listen. I could see I was upsetting the people I was closest to, pushing my friendships to breaking point.

I had to get a grip.

16

I was no longer in *Brookside*. I had been what they called a recurring character, and in 1998, when my contract was up, it wasn't renewed. Phil Redmond sat down with me and said he couldn't see anything happening with my character, Mo, for a while, so that was it. He didn't rule out asking me back at some point in the future. I was fine with it. Phil had always been decent with me and it was an amicable parting of the ways. I'd had five good years there, so it was probably a good time to move on.

In 1999, I auditioned for a guest role in the second series of Victoria Wood's comedy *Dinnerladies*. I was up for the part of the nurse, Bobbie. I remember being in the audition room with Victoria and Geoff Posner, the producer, a bowl on the table between us with little chocolate footballs in blue and red wrappers, taking a couple of the red ones and saying I was a Liverpool fan.

It was all very informal and relaxed, and I got the part. That was the good news. The bad news was that Kelly, the dog I'd got when Dannielle was little, was fifteen and her health was fading. She was a bit unsteady on her back legs and getting cysts on her stomach. After a couple of operations, the vet felt it wasn't fair to put her through more surgery and that the kindest thing was to have her put down. It was one of the hardest decisions I'd ever had to make. I couldn't bear to think of her suffering, but the prospect of putting her to sleep was upsetting for everyone. She'd been a huge part of our lives, one of the family, and we loved her. She was a great little dog, affectionate, always pleased to see us. I couldn't imagine her not being around any more.

The night before we took her to the vet, I gave her some of her favourite treats, and she slept on the bed with me and Dannielle. It broke my heart to think we were losing her. The following morning, on 9 September 1999, at the surgery, Dannielle was hysterical, and my mum was in floods of tears. I was in bits as well, and at the same time trying to be the strong one. Kelly lay on the table, good as gold, looking up at me and I stroked her and talked to her as the vet gave her the lethal injection. Seconds later, she died in my arms. That was when my legs buckled and I collapsed. Next thing, I vomited. It was horrendous. I was so attached to her.

I swore I'd never have another dog.

I threw myself into work. To me, Victoria Wood was a creative genius. Once I was working with her, I discovered she was also intensely private, one of those people you could spend three hours deep in conversation with and only realize afterwards that while you'd bared your soul, she had revealed nothing about herself. *Dinnerladies* was brilliant but intense. We rehearsed all week, ready to record at the weekend in front of a studio audience at BBC Television Centre. I'd worked like that a few years earlier on the Harry Enfield show and hadn't been at my best, but with *Dinnerladies* I was confident.

The cast included Julie Walters, Anne Reid, Thelma Barlow, Maxine Peake, who was fresh out of RADA, Shobna Gulati, who went on to play Sunita in *Coronation Street*, Sue Cleaver, Sue Devaney . . . and Celia Imrie. I got really close to Celia, who was kind hearted, good natured, talented and eccentric. She became one of the most important figures in my life and helped me in every way. I always said she was one of God's children, decent, someone who always had time for you, no matter how busy she was with work or whatever. A few years after *Dinnerladies*, she came to Liverpool and appeared in a short film of mine.

Doing that one series of *Dinnerladies* was a fantastic experience. My family and some of my friends came down from Liverpool and Widnes for the studio recordings every week. In October 1999, the weekend Dannielle was celebrating her eighteenth birthday with a party at Planet Hollywood, loads of people came down. Dannielle was mad about Steps and Mariah Carey and, as it happened, both were in the building appearing on other shows at the same time as we were recording *Dinnerladies*. I got H from Steps to sing 'Happy Birthday', and when we bumped into Mariah in the dressing-room corridor Dannielle got a photo with her and was made up. Of course, she had to push her luck, and started telling the singer about a gay friend of hers, John Gannon. 'He says you're the only woman he'd sleep with,' she said. 'If I get him on the phone, will you have a word with him?'

Mariah couldn't really say no, although, as you'd expect, John didn't believe for a second that the woman with the American accent on the other end of the phone was his idol, so he told her where to go and hung up.

It was great for me to be part of a high-profile, successful series like *Dinnerladies*. When the first series aired in 1998 it won the award for Best New TV Comedy at the British Comedy Awards and got a BAFTA nomination for Best Comedy Programme or Series.

It's funny how once you start having a bit of success, landing roles in hit TV shows, people seem to think you just woke up one day and got a job. I wish. In the last twenty-five years I've probably done more than three hundred auditions, including the *Dinnerladies* one, and not got a lot of the jobs I was up for. It's the name of the game and you learn to live with it. You have to. I'm better at dealing with disappointment now than I used to be, but I won't pretend it doesn't hurt when you don't get a role you really want.

When I was starting out, I pushed and slogged and did everything I could to get work. It wasn't always easy to get to London to audition, but I moved heaven and earth to do it. I auditioned for some of the biggest casting directors in the world and went up for all kinds of things, from the Helena Bonham Carter film *The Wings of the Dove*, to Trevor Nunn's *Les Misérables*. Usually, there wasn't time to make much of an impression. You were either what they wanted or you weren't. You'd look to camera, show them your profile, pull a face, hold up your hands, deliver a line or two, and that was it.

Thirty seconds later you'd be out the door and, in my case, heading to the station for the train back to Liverpool. For the first ten years, my agent was Shane Collins and then it was Sarah Spear at Curtis Brown, and the diversity of work I've done through both of them has been phenomenal.

With acting there's no certainty, no security, no guarantee of success. I've worked with many talented actors who couldn't make a career out of it for one reason or another. You need determination, self-belief, a thick enough skin to cope with rejection, huge reserves of perseverance. When there's no money coming in for weeks or months on end, you need to be able to get by and trust you'll turn things around. I would beg, borrow, pawn things to keep going. I've been skint loads of times. Then again, even when I had money, I was skint. I always managed to scrape by somehow, and no matter how hard up I got, I never bummed off the State and claimed unemployment benefit. That's something I'm proud of.

17

After *Dinnerladies*, back in Widnes I was teaching drama, working with a bunch of talented kids, running classes in a factory on Ditton Road on Thursday nights and doing private coaching at home at the weekend. A few of my students were outstanding and went on to study at RADA and the Central School of Speech and Drama in London. One of the girls who trained with me for a couple of years, Nicola Roberts, ended up in Girls Aloud.

Dannielle had moved back to Liverpool and was sharing a flat in Huskisson Street, two doors away from where we used to live, and I was on my own. I missed her and even though the house felt odd, empty without Kelly, I couldn't even think about having another dog.

I started doing consultancy for a company called Community Integrated Care, who worked with people with all kinds of special needs. There were children with severe disabilities, elderly dementia sufferers, others with learning disabilities, mental-health issues, autism. Some needed round-the-clock care, others were able to manage independently with a bit of extra support. CIC ran clubs and what-have-you, teaching arts and crafts and practical skills like cookery. I got involved doing drama, workshops and shows. I was making good money and kept up my teaching in Widnes as well as slotting in the odd bit of TV work, including the Ray Winstone drama, *Tough Love*.

For years I'd had problems with impacted wisdom teeth. I had a phobia about the dentist and kept putting off going until the pain became unbearable. In the end, I was in Tenerife on holiday with Rachael in 2001 and was in such agony I was demented, butting the walls trying to get relief.

My mum flew me home early and I got an emergency appointment with a dentist. That night, what started as a dull ache ended up with one side of my face so badly swollen you couldn't see my eye. My mouth was infected and I spent the night in Whiston Hospital, where I was treated with antibiotics and morphine for the pain. The next morning, I was transferred to the Royal Liverpool Hospital and kept in for a week while they stabilized me. Their main worry was that I would develop septicaemia. Being diabetic and fat and having high blood pressure only served to complicate things. Basically, at thirty-eight, I had the body and constitution of someone twice my age. I was a mess.

Once they discharged me, I went to have my wisdom teeth out and ended up with fifteen stitches in one side of my mouth and twenty in the other. By then, I had abscesses and they became infected. My mouth was in a right old state. I was staying at my mum's and felt something go pop. What came out of my mouth was like something out of *The Exorcist*. My mum nearly passed out. I was whipped straight back into the Royal and spent the next eight weeks there, on morphine, hooked up to drips that pumped antibiotics and saline into my system. I was really poorly.

Every day Mum and Dad and Dannielle would visit. Rachael was always there. She'd sit with me at night if I couldn't sleep and we'd go to the canteen in the basement, which stayed open until the early hours of the morning. Some nights, it was filled with scallies having a fag, swapping stories, and smackheads getting out the silver foil, chasing the dragon. Odd bits of conversation would drift our way.

'I got shot last week.'

'Oh, did yer? I stabbed my fella and now he's cut me arm open.'

It was another world, one I was desperate to get away from. I wanted to go home, but every time I asked, I was told the infection hadn't cleared and if they discharged me too soon, with the added complication of my diabetes and blood pressure, there was every chance I'd be readmitted – into intensive care next time.

The weeks went by in a blur of pain relief, visitors coming and going. I drifted in and out of groggy, sedative-induced sleep. When I was finally allowed home, I was warned it would take at least a couple of months to recuperate and adjust to life again after such a long time sedated and more or less bedridden on morphine.

I had no job, no money coming in, just the odd drama

workshop. I was living off my father. The only work commitment I remember having was a minor role in a short film Ricky Tomlinson was doing, *Five Ways John Wayne Didn't Die*, directed by Martin Wallace. Jarvis Cocker from Pulp was in it as well, and it was being shot at ... the Royal Liverpool Hospital. I'm surprised they didn't name a ward after me, the amount of time I spent there. I'd sold my house in Belvoir Road, at the wrong time, apparently, and lost thousands on it. When I left hospital I went to live in a two-bedroom house in Severn Close, still in Widnes. Mum and Dad helped decorate, Rachael and Dannielle sanded the floors, and between us we got it looking nice.

All the time I was in hospital I had wanted to go home, then once I got there I was in a bad way, thoroughly depressed. Dannielle was at college and living in Liverpool and I was on my own, which probably wasn't ideal after weeks in hospital being looked after. It got so I didn't want to leave the house. Mum and Dad would bring groceries and I'd stay cooped up indoors in a state of high anxiety, convinced everybody hated me. For a while I experienced what they called phantom pain where the infection had been, which was something the doctors had said might happen. I was on prescription painkillers, taking as many as twelve a day. Mentally, I was all over the place. I got it into my head that moths were trying to get into the house and the thought of it freaked me out. One night I rang my dad in the early hours, hysterical, because a moth was fluttering around the bedroom. Bless him, he got out of bed and drove the thirty miles from Anfield to deal with it. I ended up so paranoid I nailed down the bedroom windows to keep the moths out.

My mind became a dark place. I'd sit watching TV and out of the corner of my eye would see giant spiders scuttling across the floor. I didn't mention this to anyone. I began to see the television as something sinister, a means of keeping me under surveillance, and I suspected my parents of somehow spying on me through the screen. All this may have had something to do with the fact I'd been on high doses of morphine for several weeks and was still taking strong painkillers. At night, instead of going to bed, I'd stay up writing endless to-do lists. I wasn't sleeping and I definitely wasn't thinking straight. I felt an absolute failure.

As usual, at the heart of everything, was my weight. I felt horribly insecure, trapped in a cycle of eating too much, getting bigger and bigger, and not able to do anything about it. I wasn't drinking, I wasn't taking drugs. Food was the only crutch I had left. I hated being fat. It was socially unacceptable. It made me aggressive and defensive and hostile. At 5ft 1in tall I was starting to look like Humpty Dumpty. I kept thinking: *I'm lonely, therefore I'll eat. I'm lonely because I eat. I might as well eat because I'm lonely.*

On and on. It became a vicious circle.

My doctor suggested a support group for compulsive eaters and sent me to a clinic on London Road in Liverpool. I went a few times but, if anything, it made me more depressed. They weighed me, took my measurements, and talked to me about weight-loss programmes. Not meaning to sound ungrateful, but they weren't telling me anything I didn't already know. I was fat because I was eating too much, eating the wrong things. It was stating the obvious to say I needed to cut down. I understood about calories and healthy eating and, when I put my mind to it, I was able to lose weight, although never as much as I wanted to, and I certainly couldn't keep it off. That was the problem. What I really needed to work out was *why* food had become such a minefield, a means of fuelling my sense of self-hate. I needed to get to the bottom of what was going on inside me that meant I had a need to eat and eat and couldn't stop. Basically, I needed more than a few well-intentioned tips on healthy eating.

I was willing to try anything, including slimming pills. For a while was on Tenuate Dospan, an appetite suppressant. They were all the rage. I knew a lot of people who were taking them. I found they made me hyper. I'd be up at four in the morning, wide awake, doing the hoovering. Unfortunately, they didn't help me lose weight. I tried something called Orlistat, little blue tablets that work by stopping your body from absorbing fat. The idea is you pass the undigested fat when you go to the loo. They were horrendous, played havoc with my insides, and had me rushing to the toilet. No thanks.

18

In early 2002, things began to pick up again when I started seeing a guy and got a part in a play called *Mum's The Word*, which meant a nine-month national tour with the Scottish theatre company Robert C. Kelly. I was dead excited about it, really happy. The only cloud on the horizon was that my dad had been poorly with emphysema and ended up in hospital for a couple of weeks. It was hard to know how bad he really was because he spent most of the time loudly insisting he was fine.

'Bloody fuss about nothing,' he'd say whenever anyone showed any concern for him.

It was almost unheard of for my dad to be ill. He was one of those fit, energetic types, always on the go, still grafting hard even though he was approaching seventy. As he'd got older, his language skills had come to the fore and he was working with foreign students, doing a lot of travelling. It was a standing joke in the family that whenever you called on him there'd be people there who could barely speak a word of English. He'd always been musical and had a good voice, and in his spare time he loved getting up and singing, doing karaoke. There were no signs of him growing old, slowing down, none that I could see, anyway, not until the summer of 2000 when he'd had a bad accident.

Coming out of the bookies on Oakfield Road in Anfield, near where he lived, in a hurry to get home to watch a Euro 2000 game on TV, he ran across the road without looking and a taxi hit him and sent him flying. He landed in a mangled heap. I got a call to say he was in the Royal, and when I got there, he was on a stretcher in the corridor, cuts all over his face. He'd broken his leg and hip, and his hand had swollen to the size of a rugby ball. I was hysterical, crying my eyes out. It was the first time he had ever been in hospital. Up until then, I'd always seen him as strong and solid, invincible. All of a sudden I had to face facts that my sprightly, fit father was vulnerable. Of course, he was his usual stop-making-a-fuss self, insisting he was OK – which was clearly rubbish, since he was about to go into theatre for surgery. Despite his injuries, there was not so much as a murmur of complaint from him, while I was a sobbing, weeping mess.

'Dad, is there anything I can do? Is there anything I can get you?'

He had a think. 'I wouldn't mind a pint of Guinness.'

He had a hip replacement and spent four weeks in hospital. From day one he was a bugger and drove the nurses insane. 'I'm fit and fine,' he'd say. 'Let me get bloody home.'

Never in a million years would he have admitted the

accident had an impact on his confidence, but I truly think it did. Physically, he bounced back without so much as a hobble but, mentally, he was less sure of himself, more conscious of his own mortality. I thought so, anyway. He knew he was to blame for what had happened, that he'd lost concentration and been careless, which was totally out of character for him. The taxi driver who had hit him hadn't stood a chance. In the aftermath, it began to dawn on my father that he might be getting on, growing old. I didn't like hearing him say it.

'You're sixty-eight – that's not old,' I'd say. 'That's middle-aged.'

He'd give me a wry look. 'How many middle-aged people getting on for a hundred and forty do you know then, Grimble?'

In 2002, after his bout of emphysema, he came to stay with me in Widnes. All my life, he'd been the one taking care of me, and now it was the other way round. I gave him my bedroom and slept on the couch downstairs. He used to bang on the floor and I'd go up and sit on the bed and have a fag with him, talk about anything and everything.

'You should write a book,' he said one day. 'You've packed a lot in, it would be interesting. Just watch your spelling.'

Sometimes, I'd get upset and hug him, tell him I loved him. It was August, the weather was good, and he sat out in the garden most days with his feet up. I ran an extension cable from the living room and brought the TV and DVD player outside and we watched the same films over and over: *The Green Mile, Saving Private Ryan, The Godfather*. It took me back to when I was little and the two of us watched musicals like

The Wizard of Oz, The Sound of Music and *West Side Story* together.

After three wonderful weeks, he went back to his flat in Liverpool and I started work on *Mum's The Word*. A couple of weeks later it was Dannielle's twenty-first and I threw a party for her. My dad didn't come. He made light of it. 'It's not my scene,' he said.

We were also having a family dinner and he said he would be at that, so I didn't think anything of it. Later, I wondered if skipping the party was a sign he hadn't been feeling well.

The play was going well and I'd got friendly with one of the other actresses, Beverley Callard, Liz McDonald in *Coronation Street*. Wherever I was on tour, I spoke to my dad every day. In Birmingham, we played the Hippodrome and I was booked into the Holiday Inn. The guy I was seeing had driven up to spend a couple of hours with me, and once he'd gone I phoned my dad and said I was going to watch the Bette Midler film *Beaches*, in bed. I'd always loved the soundtrack, especially 'The Glory of Love'.

'Remember how you used to sing it to me?' I said.

'You've got to laugh a little, cry a little,' he sang.

I felt a lump in my throat.

'Oh, don't start crying,' he said. 'You and your sentimental dross.'

I could picture the look on his face, smiling and rolling his eyes at the same time. I went, 'Don't lie, Dad, you used to sit with me and watch *The Sound of Music, and* enjoy it.'

We gabbed on for a bit.

I told him the play was going well and I was having a good time. 'I love you, Dad.'

'I know you do, Grimble.' It always made me smile when he called me that. 'Now, go and watch your film ...'

It was the last time we spoke.

The next day, 16 October, I got the train to Manchester and a friend, Paul Burke, met me at Piccadilly Station. I'd got to know Paul and his other half, Jackie, through my good friend Vinny Davies. We were going to have lunch with some friends at their house nearby and my fella was meeting us there. On the way, my mobile rang. It was my mum.

All she managed to say was, 'Chris,' before breaking down.

I was frantic. 'What's happened? What's wrong?'

'Your dad's dead.'

I was hysterical, deranged. In the time it took for my mum to break the news, my world collapsed around me. When I got to my friends' place, my fella was waiting and we jumped in the car and drove to Liverpool, speeding all the way, straight to my dad's flat. Mum and Dannielle and my brother, Simon, were there. The day before, Dad had driven some Russian exchange students to Blackpool. When I had spoken to him a few hours later he was fine, his usual self, a bit tired maybe, but nothing I'd picked up on. There was no sign that anything was wrong. I couldn't make sense of it. How could he be dead?

For the last couple of years he'd been living in sheltered accommodation, and when he hadn't appeared that morning, the warden had checked on him and found him still in bed. He'd had a massive heart attack and died during the night. A half-smoked cigarette was in the ashtray next to the bed. The crossword he'd been doing and his pen were on the little side table. I picked them up and put them in my bag. I was in a terrible state, absolutely inconsolable, crying my eyes out. I couldn't believe he'd gone. I couldn't stand to be near my mum or Dannielle or our Simon. That night, I got my bloke to drive me back to Birmingham and I sat up all night in my hotel room with Bev Callard, wailing.

How I didn't start drinking again, I'll never know.

Mum's The Word got an understudy for me but I wasn't about to bail out. I'd inherited my father's drive. The next night I went on stage in a comedy with red, puffy, swollen eyes and, somehow, with enormous support from my fellow cast members, got through it. I knew it was what my dad would have wanted. I could almost hear him saying. 'Get back to work, Christina.'

It's a funny thing, acting, pretending to be someone you're not. I'd been doing it my whole life, one way or another. In the weeks after the death of my father, it became a means of escape and I took refuge in it. On stage, I was able to put the grief I felt to one side and inhabit a character that wasn't stricken and crying. For a couple of hours each night I became somebody else, and the routine, the discipline of work, especially with people who were kind and supportive around me, helped.

Away from work, I was a complete wreck.

After going back on stage that first night, the following day I got a taxi over to Liverpool and went to the funeral home. I sat with my dad and combed his hair, put a flower in the coffin. He looked peaceful, asleep. I had never felt as bad in my life. I cried and cried for days until it got to the point where my eyes were so sore and bulbous I couldn't open them. A doctor came to the hotel and said I had something called greasy tears. All the crying had made my eyes inflamed and infected.

I carried on with *Mum's The Word* and didn't miss a single performance, although the days went by in a haze of tears and hurt and disbelief and anger and madness. I could not understand other people carrying on with their lives as normal when my father was dead. I felt his loss every waking moment. Ours hadn't always been an easy relationship, probably because we were so alike, both very opinionated. When we argued, we'd bawl at each other. We were close and he was always there, though, someone I could talk to about anything – and I did, almost every day of my life.

I was in no sense ready to lose him. In a way, I was selfish in my grief because I felt it was *my* loss, not anyone else's. It was all about me and how I felt and I didn't acknowledge the impact on my mum or Simon or Dannielle. On a train with Bev Callard, the sound of people around us in the carriage, nothing to do with us, talking and laughing, almost sent me over the edge. I wanted to scream at them to shut up. All I could think was, *My dad died four days ago!*

Every day, I went into the funeral home and sat with him, talked to him, and my fella came with me. He promised my dad he'd look after me. A couple of days after Dad died, I got my first Best Actress nomination in the Manchester Evening News Awards for *Mum's The Word*. It felt meaningless because he wasn't there to see it. Everything I'd done, all I'd achieved, was down to him. He had pushed me, made me believe I could be anything I wanted. He had given me the drive and determination to succeed. Every ounce of ambition I had, all my tenacity, came from him. It seemed wrong that, just as I was getting some acknowledgement, it was too late for him to see it. The nomination was as much his as mine. I put it in his coffin.

On the day of the funeral, I travelled to the crematorium in the car with my grandad, John. The last few years had been hard on him. My nan, Leonie, had suffered from Alzheimer's for ten years before her death in 1997, and been in and out of hospital. She veered from being sharp and lucid to having no idea who anyone was. When she got confused, she sometimes wandered off. Keeping an eye on her must have been a huge strain on my grandad. At one point she went missing and turned up in London, at Euston Station, with money sewn into the lining of her coat. When the police picked her up, she told them the Germans were coming and that she'd had to take her money out of the bank for safe-keeping.

In the funeral car, my grandad sat straight-backed, digni-fied. I couldn't help thinking how frail and hollow he looked. He had already buried his wife and his youngest son, Ronnie. Now he had lost another son. Ask any parent, and they'll tell you the last thing they want to do is outlive their children. At Springwood Crematorium, I held myself together to deliver the eulogy but, as my dad's coffin slid away out of sight, my legs went and I collapsed.

I could not imagine life going on without him.

I started having panic attacks again, really bad ones, like I had when I'd been drinking. I couldn't get my breath and my heart would go like the clappers. I knew about breathing into a paper bag and keeping calm and rubbing my wrists but it didn't always help. I'd be gasping for air and then I'd start panicking about my blood pressure, which was already high, thinking it wasn't a panic attack I was having, it was a heart attack. A couple of times I called an ambulance.

In the months after losing my dad, I felt as if my life was slipping away and got really ill. I couldn't get over his death. I was absolutely lost without him. I pushed my family away, pushed away my friends. I cried all the time. Not having him any more was unbearable. The drink and drugs I would once have leaned on in times of crisis were gone and all that was left was food. I was eating too much, becoming carb-obsessed, getting fatter, hating what I was doing to myself. The more depressed I got, the more consumed with food I became.

Mum's The Word came to an end and on an impulse, I decided to make a fresh start. I cleared off so fast it was less like a move and more like a flit. I packed my things and took off, moved into a lovely penthouse flat in Duke Street, in Liverpool, all in the space of about two weeks. In January 2003, I had my fortieth birthday and threw myself into work again.

19

Liverpool was in the throes of change, massive regeneration
transforming the city. I hardly recognized the place, it was
such a hive of activity, with bars and bistros and restaurants,
all packed out. Old, falling-down warehouses had been given
a new lease of life as luxury apartments. Everywhere you
looked there were penthouses springing up. Where I was, in
Duke Street, was right in the middle of town. From the deck-
ing on the terrace outside my living room, I could see both
cathedrals and Percy Street, where I'd grown up. I had a real
sense of being back where I belonged. I had my hair extensions done and my nails, and even though I was getting
bigger I began to feel better about myself than I had for a
while. I was teaching drama in Hope Street, right next to my
old school, Blackburne House, and had a company called
DSTM with Dean Sullivan, who'd played Jimmy Corkhill in
Brookside. My students were getting into *Brookside* and

Hollyoaks and the Danny Boyle film *Millions*, and I was becoming known as someone who was political and outspoken about Liverpool's urban renewal, serving on boards, speaking at rallies.

Dannielle moved into a flat in Hudson Gardens across from where I was living and, in lots of ways, life was good, although everything was coloured by the loss of my dad. I decided to make a short film in his honour and wrote a trilogy based around the lives of taxi drivers. One thing I had never done was learn to drive, so I spent huge amounts of time in taxis. I was thinking about it recently, working out where my money went, and a lot of it was on taxi fares. No word of a lie, over the years, I reckon I must have spent about £250,000 on cabs.

The first film in the trilogy, *Reuben, Don't Take Your Love To Town*, was the story of a cab driver whose wife of twenty-odd years didn't want to have sex with him any more. When his mates down the cab office tell him to get it elsewhere, he's not interested. It's his wife he loves and wants things back the way they used to be.

I set about raising money for the *Reuben* film which, being a romantic, I'd decided to shoot on 35mm, like a proper feature. I raised £140,000 from various philanthropists, including Gary Millar, who's now Lord Mayor of Liverpool, and his partner, Steve McFarlane. They invited me and Dean for dinner at their penthouse on the dock, I pitched the idea, and they wrote a cheque for £10,000 there and then. I arranged a meeting with a Scouse Cypriot entrepreneur with a string of properties and restaurants in the city. We became great friends and he loved the idea of a film that would be shot locally and show Liverpool at its best. He chipped in £50,000, and put me in touch with a friend of his in the Cypriot business community, who also contributed. Their faith in me and their generosity made all the difference. I was upfront about the precarious nature of the film industry and said I couldn't make any promises about how we'd do. Barring death and the taxman nothing was guaranteed, was how I put it. Nobody minded. Everyone who put money into the film believed in it.

I got together an amazing cast, including Celia Imrie, who did it for nothing, and Johnny Vegas. Neil Fitzmaurice – Ray-Von in the Channel 4 comedy, *Phoenix Nights* – was Reuben and my mate Kerry Williams played his wife, Frances. I also cast some of my students. Dean Sullivan directed and we shot our first scene with Neil Fitzmaurice on the steps of the Catholic cathedral on 16 October 2003, a year to the day after my dad had died. It was glorious weather. 'Oh, Dad's brought the sun out,' I said as we set up. We shot the film over two weeks and produced a twelve-minute short. During the edit the money ran out and I needed an extra £30,000 or so to get it all done, which a friend came up with. We took *Reuben* to the film festival in Cannes and, courtesy of Panavision, had a boat and an amazing few days on the Riviera. We got nominations for Best Short Film at several festivals, including Cannes, London, Sundance and Barcelona. My dad would have been proud.

Things were going well professionally, but my health wasn't great. I was injecting insulin three times a day but didn't always manage my diabetes as well as I needed to, and I'd end up having a hypo. I was on my own in the apartment in

Duke Street one day and felt sick and peculiar and suddenly, boom, I collapsed. It's almost like you're drunk, delirious and unsteady, out of it. I managed to get to my friend Nicky's flat next door but she wasn't there and I ended up rousing one of the other neighbours, who called an ambulance. I had a few of those episodes, usually when I was on some stupid fad diet or other, living on baked potatoes and tinned tomatoes or something because I'd cut out all fat, which I've since learned your body needs. Each time I had a hypo, I ended up back in the Royal Liverpool for anything from a few days to a week until my blood-sugar levels were back where they were supposed to be.

I was starting to audition for different bits and bobs of telly. If you'd met me back then, you'd have thought I had everything going for me, apart from the fact I was enormous. As was so often the case, though, I was putting on a front that hid what was really going on: the grief I felt over losing my dad was as bad as ever. I didn't want to go on without him. I've never been suicidal in terms of sitting with a bottle of vodka and a load of pills thinking about ending it all, but for a while I really didn't want to live. In bed, I'd cry and talk out loud, ask God to let me die. I told myself that, at twenty-one, Dannielle would be fine, my mum would be fine. All I wanted was to be with my dad. It was obvious I wasn't getting better, and my mate Rachael was frightened for me. It made her frantic that I couldn't move on and she urged me to get proper help. I went to my GP, told him how I felt, and he arranged for an assessment at Park Lane, the unit in Liverpool that handles mental-health problems. I saw two psychiatrists and was told that the most likely treatment would be sessions with a therapist, an hour a week for eight or sixteen weeks, depending on how bad my depression was. When it came to it, they decided I needed long-term help, consisting of Cognitive Behavioural Therapy, two hours a week for the next two years.

Every week I saw my therapist and spilled my guts about what was going on inside my head. I talked about the death of my father, the gaping wound it had left in my life, and the sense I would never be able to recover. I opened up about being fat and never managing to get my eating under control. Things that had gone on in my childhood came up – being bullied at junior school, always feeling the odd one out, lying about where I came from because I wanted to fit in. I told him how I'd reinvented myself and become a scally and a fighter. For hours and hours, week after week, I talked and he listened. It all came out. Everything.

20

My self-esteem was as low as it could get – even with the therapy. Inside my head was a dark place. The more depressed I got, the more insular I became and lacking in motivation. Where money was concerned, I was totally irresponsible. I fell out with Rachael. I fell out with a lot of people. I regret neglecting my friendships – not just letting things slide, but pushing away the very people who had done the most for me over the years, career-wise and financially, in terms of advice and encouragement and a place to stay when I needed one. Funnily enough, when I was drinking and dabbling in drugs, I was probably a lot more consistent in my friendships than after I'd cleaned up my act.

I've got a list of people I feel I let down badly. My mum's on it, right at the top. Rachael Lindsay, Jonathan Harvey, Kathy Burke, Jimmy Mulville, Joy Blakeman. Wendy Harris, the director at the Rathbone, who lived in the flat above me when I was starting out. There are probably a few more, but those are the ones that stick out. Dannielle would say she should be on the list too, but she's the one person I never neglected, no matter what.

I couldn't break the cycle of dieting, losing a couple of stone, putting it back on, and I couldn't get a handle on my spending. The *Reuben* film had left me owing a lot of money, and at the same time I wasn't earning what I needed to make ends meet. It became impossible to find £1,500 a month for my rent on the Duke Street penthouse and I had to give it up and move into a smaller apartment.

In the middle of all this, I went for an audition with the casting agent David Shaw for a part in a TV series, *Brief Lives*. I really wanted the job and when I got a recall I was chuffed, thinking it was in the bag. Then I didn't get it and was absolutely crushed, convinced I wasn't going to find work. David Shaw said there was a part, something small, coming up in the second series of *Shameless* on Channel 4, if I was interested. I'd seen the series when it first aired in 2004 and was blown away by the antics of the dysfunctional Gallagher family on the Chatsworth Estate in Manchester. I remember watching, thinking I'd have killed to be in it. Paul Abbott, the creator, had come up with something offbeat and original, funny and outrageous. It was brilliant telly and I don't think anyone was surprised when the first series won three Royal Television Society awards, including Best Drama. When David Shaw mentioned it, though, I was so low and demoralized after not getting *Brief Lives* that I couldn't see the point in going for it. I really didn't know if it was worth it, not for such a small part. In the end I decided to have a go and auditioned for Dearbhla Walsh, a director on the show, for the part of Mimi Maguire. Mimi was only going to feature in a couple of episodes and they hadn't quite worked out how they wanted her to be played. They were looking at a few different actresses. When Dearbhla asked me how I saw the character, I knew exactly how I would play her.

'She's Scouse, orange, brassy, in your face. She'd slit your throat for three pounds fifty. She's got hair extensions and acrylic nails and thinks she's a WAG but she's too fat and old to be one.'

I got the part.

I was made up, not so much about playing Mimi, but because it was a Paul Abbott show and to me he was a total genius. That was the joy for me of landing the part. I wouldn't have cared what it was or whether it was a single line in one episode, it was *Paul Abbott* and I idolized him and his work.

The first episode I was in was the one where Mimi's daughter, Mandy, was pregnant and everyone thought Ian Gallagher was the father, although of course Ian being with Mandy was a cover for him being gay, and it was his brother Lip who was really the dad. All very complicated with lots of potential for misunderstandings, in true *Shameless* style. It was a great episode for me. You got a real sense of Mimi as a terrifying woman, the kind you wouldn't ever want to cross. At one point she had a knife to Ian's throat and, when Lip came clean and said the baby was actually his and the engagement party descended into a mass brawl, she head-butted him. The first scene I actually shot was the Maguires going to meet the Gallaghers, their future in-laws, in a limo. I wasn't overcome with nerves or anything but I don't think I'd really connected with Mimi at that point, and to me, it showed on screen. I felt I'd not made the best of starts, that it wasn't the finest bit of acting on my part. No one else had a problem, but I knew I hadn't done a great job.

At the wrap party at the end of the series, I had a chat with the producers, George Faber and Charlie Pattinson. About ten years earlier, in 1994, I'd worked with them on a Screen Two film for the BBC, *Sin Bin*, alongside Kathy Burke and Pete Postlethwaite, so we already knew each other.

'We'll have you back next year,' George said.

With that first dodgy scene, which no one else had even noticed, well and truly behind me, I had a really good feeling about Mimi. 'That would be amazing, I'd love to,' I said.

In 2005, I was doing other work, including the BBC drama *Fingersmith*, with Elaine Cassidy, Sally Hawkins, Imelda Staunton and Charles Dance. I also did a play at the Everyman in Liverpool, *The Morris*, about a female dance troupe. The writer, Helen Blakeman, was the sister of Joy Blakeman, who I'd worked with on *The Long Day Closes*. I played Lily and got good reviews. According to *The Stage*, 'Tina Malone glories in the role of morose Lily, the supposed leader, and creates a sullen, silent monster. Suddenly she lets go with the bellowing voice of an overbearing boor. Malone's forceful character makes a highlight performance.' It was a great play but it wasn't a happy time for me because of my weight and the relationship I was in. I clashed with the director, Indhu Rubasingham, as well.

The following year I was back on *Shameless* and did a couple more episodes in series three. From series four on,

Mimi and the Maguires were in every episode. I loved her and it was a joy going to work, being part of an incredible series.

The cast and crew of *Shameless* were friendly and welcoming from the off. You always hear actors on soaps like *Emmerdale* and *Coronation Street* say it's like one big, happy family, and to an extent I'm sure it is, but I know people who've worked on those shows who say there's a definite hierarchy. On *Shameless*, there wasn't. We really were a family, a very happy one. Going in, I was nervous and at the same time incredibly excited to be joining such a great cast. It can be odd going into a series, a bit intimidating, so it helps when people go out of their way to ease you in. David Threlfall, who played Frank Gallagher, couldn't have been nicer. The young lads, Ged Kearns (Ian Gallagher), Elliott Tittensor (Carl Gallagher) and Jody Latham (Lip Gallagher), were great. There were so many exceptional individuals, including some wonderful women: Maggie O'Neill, Anne-Marie Duff, Maxine Peake, Gillian Kearney. I already knew Marjorie Yates, from working with her a few years before on *The Long Day Closes*.

When I'd first started at *Brookside*, in 1993, I was the new girl, inexperienced, and made sure I was well prepared on my first day. I'd learnt the script and had a scene with an actress who knew the ropes inside out. For years, I'd dreamt of being in *Brookside*, plagued the life out of Phil Redmond, and finally I'd made it. It was a huge thing for me. That first day on set, surrounded by new people, adrenalin pumping, I was eager, wanting to make a great impression. The actress I was working with practically ignored me. She was so dismissive. Not once did she ask if I'd like to run my lines or offer me the least bit of encouragement. She didn't give me the fucking time of day. All she did was moan about how shit everything was and complained because she had to be somewhere else that night. We shot the scene and got it in the can without her exchanging a single nicety. So fucking rude.

I vowed I'd never treat anybody I worked with like that, and I never have. Ask anyone who came into *Shameless* who it was who went out of their way to make them feel at home, show them where they could get a coffee, take them to the canteen, the Green Room ... they'll tell you it was me. I know that when you're young and starting out it can be deflating if someone's unfriendly. I also know that, on long-running dramas, it's not always that people are being rude, more that the schedule is so tight there isn't time to chat. What I've realized is that the higher up the scale you go, the more friendly people tend to be. I worked with Ray Winstone and Michael Maloney on *Henry VIII* in 2003 and they couldn't have been nicer. On *Fingersmith*, Imelda Staunton and Charles Dance were lovely. Then you get some knob-head on *Brookside*. I saw her on TV, doing some shitty advert, and couldn't help thinking it was a case of reaping what you sow.

21

When I first started in *Shameless*, I was living in a small apartment in Beetham Tower, in Liverpool, and as usual was battling with my weight. Every morning, our Lynn would pick me up before six on her way to work and drop me at the Crowne Plaza and I'd have a swim followed by a workout. Five days a week, a good friend, Lindsay Inglesby, a choreographer who'd been one of my drama students, would spend an hour with me doing dance, body pump, ball work, all kinds of cardiovascular exercise. With all those intense swim and gym sessions I was doing, you'd think the weight would be falling off. It wasn't. I was getting bigger and I couldn't understand why. It was thoroughly depressing. It seemed whatever I did, however disciplined I was, I couldn't shift the weight. I went to see a doctor privately in Formby and he suspected I had something called Cushing's Syndrome. I'd never heard of it. I went home and looked it up on the internet and it was like looking in the mirror. All the pictures of people with Cushing's were exactly like me – big moon face, huge eyes, rotund body, thin legs sticking out, what they called a camel's hump on the back.

Initially, I was referred to the Linda McCartney Centre, which freaked me out as it's a cancer unit. After running some tests, I was diagnosed with borderline Cushing's. In America, Cushing's is known as the obesity tumour. With this particular condition, apparently, you develop a tumour on the pituitary gland at the front of the brain that sends a signal to your adrenal glands to produce excessive amounts of the stress hormone, cortisol. All that cortisol in your system affects your metabolism and plays havoc with your weight, which was why I was getting bigger, no matter what I did. I was beginning to despair of ever getting my weight under control. My blood pressure was sky high and I was at an increased risk of having a heart attack or stroke.

Once again, I was readmitted to the Royal Liverpool, this time for three weeks, and put on beta blockers. Nothing about what was going on with my health surprised me. While the work side of my life was phenomenal, it was a different story at home – I had been in and out of a bad relationship for a while, and it was taking its toll. No wonder my body was flooded with cortisol – I was stressed out and anxious more or less the whole time.

The more I thought about my life, the more depressed I became.

At times, I arrived for work in Manchester at the start of a twelve-hour shift and sat in the make-up chair trying to make sense of what was going on at home. I'd see my reflection in the mirror and it would be like looking at someone I didn't know. I knew I was blessed to be playing such a great character and earning good money, able to go on holiday, treat my friends. I also knew what a fucking mess my life was.

It may sound crazy, but I'd reached the point where I truly believed the only way out would be if I was dead. I played a hard-faced drug dealer, a woman one critic called 'Tony Soprano in a frock'. Mimi was terrifying: foul-mouthed, fearless, vile, violent. Cross her and you'd know about it. But Mimi was my only escape from the rest of my life. When we were busy on *Shameless*, I was more her than I was me. I'd leave the house early, often just after six in the morning, and wrap at seven in the evening. In my lunch break I'd usually be doing an interview or learning lines. A typical working week for me, taking into account personal appearances – opening shops and what-have-you at the weekend – and teaching drama, could be anything from eighty to a hundred hours. At the earliest I'd get home around seven-thirty and then there'd be lines to learn for the following day, pages of dialogue that could take two, three hours to get my head round. The writers were constantly making changes, which would come through on different coloured paper. You almost needed a degree to keep track of things. The pink pages that replaced the green ones would become blue or purple or yellow as more and more amendments came through. I didn't mind because I enjoyed being pushed to the limit and knew all those changes were about making sure the show was the best it could be. I wanted to be busy, to have no space to think about other stuff.

I was in my element playing Mimi. It's rare to get a gritty

part like that written for a woman. Sometimes, I felt her spilling over into real life. For a few months I was living in a lovely apartment block in Manchester, one of those buildings with balconies running around the inside and a mezzanine floor overlooking a fountain in the lobby. It was gorgeous. What I hadn't realized was that it was full of students and at night there was no peace. I might as well have been in Ibiza. One night around eleven o'clock when the noise became unbearable, I went to see what was going on and found the balcony crowded with people drinking and chatting, laughing, making a proper racket. Someone had their door open and music was thumping out. Nothing I'd want to listen to. I'd had enough and let rip.

'Fucking shut *up*! Get in your own flats and drink – just fuck off!'

They all turned and looked, incredulous, and someone said, 'Oh my God, it's Mimi.'

'Just fuck off, the lot of you!' I stormed back inside and gave the door a good slam. Outside, it went really quiet.

Going back to when I'd seen Ray Winstone in *Scum* in 1979 and Gary Oldman in *The Firm* ten years later – both brilliant films directed by Alan Clarke – I'd wanted to do something edgy, controversial. I never thought I'd get the chance. Until Mimi came along. As an actor, you have to feel an empathy with your character, no matter how much of a villain or what-have-you they might be. It's the only way to make whoever it is you're playing feel real. Every actor has their own thoughts on how best to get under the skin of the person they're playing. Some go to more extreme lengths than others. It helped on *Shameless* that the writing was so

good. Ed McCardie and Jimmy Dowdall came up with wonderful scripts. I loved everything by Kevin Erlis and Tom
Higgins because they were Scousers and had a knack of writing in a rhythm that was just right for me, and Sarah Hooper,
who became a good friend, wrote brilliantly for me too.

I never struggled with the violent side of Mimi. I'd been in
enough fights and flare-ups when I was younger to have a
good sense of how to make those scenes convincing. Years
ago, I was in a famous club in Liverpool, the She, with
Jimmy's sister, Debbie, when a girl wearing high heels stood
on me. She didn't even notice her stiletto had cut my foot
open. It was excruciating and there was blood everywhere. I
turned on her.

'Ah, you stupid bitch!'

She spun round. 'Who do you think you are, the fucking
Queen of Sheba?'

I smacked her. She punched me. We ended up boxing on
the dance floor, kicking and punching. It was like something
out of the Wild West. Debbie was doubled up, crying with
laughter.

In Southport, I was out with my friend Lyn Smythe at the
Riverside, a huge club, chatting to a couple of guys, when a
girl we'd never seen before jumped out from behind the fruit
machine onto Lyn's back. I think one of the lads was her ex.
It erupted into a huge fight. Another girl started on me and
took a clump of hair out of my head. When she tried to
make a run for it, I grabbed the back of her dress and ripped.
The whole thing came away in my hand. She was stood in
the middle of the club in her bra and pants, trying to cover
herself, everyone in the place whooping and cheering. That

kind of stuff went on all the time. I didn't even know what half the fights were about. Sometimes, it was a case of wrong place, wrong time. I've seen so much stuff close-up that no matter where I am now, from the poshest clubs to absolute dives, I have an uncanny sense of when trouble is about to erupt.

Whenever things kicked off in the Jockey on *Shameless* it took me back to those crazy times in the bars and clubs of Liverpool and Southport. Making the fight scenes real was easy. Sometimes, the directors would say, 'You've done that before.'

The chances were I had.

In series five of *Shameless*, which aired in 2008, we did what I call the fat episode. By then, I was tightly ensconced in the part. I was also massively overweight, getting on for 19 stone, wearing hideous, baggy, unflattering, size 28 clothes. The storyline was about an old boyfriend of Mimi's, Other Paddy, coming back on the scene and putting his foot in it over how big she'd got since they'd last seen each other. He didn't even recognize her. What he said made Mimi take a long hard look at herself. It was familiar territory for me. I remember a meeting with Paul Abbott, the creator, Stephen Russell, the writer, David Threlfall, who was directing, and John Griffin, the producer, all of them tiptoeing about, nobody wanting to actually use the word 'FAT' for fear of offending me. I went out of my way to make sure everyone knew I was fine with it, since the last thing I wanted was for anyone to be uncomfortable on set.

We did a scene where Mimi looked in the mirror and then

broke down and sobbed on the bed. I thought it would be cathartic but actually it was horrendous. I was thinking, 'Oh God, this is the part of Mimi that's exactly like me.' It was really quite painful to do.

Paddy tried to console her but when he said he didn't think of her as fat she went berserk and threw him out. 'I can't believe you used the fucking F-word in my presence,' she said, furious.

This was Mimi, always so hard, showing a vulnerable side no one guessed she had. The writing was genius, poignant, and at the same time funny. When her daughter, Mandy, offered to help her lose weight, Mimi told her, 'I don't want to stop drinking or eating . . . or do any exercise . . .'

David Threlfall directed with great sensitivity. He had a knack of picking up on whatever insecurities you had and he knew I was suffering over my size. I couldn't even stand to watch myself on screen or look at the rushes, and he was aware of it without me having to say anything. We were very lucky with the directors on *Shameless*. Laurence Till was very theatrical but real and kind, and trusted you to know what you were doing. Gordon Anderson was intense, gave the emotional stuff real weight, and worked brilliantly with me and Michael Taylor, who played Billy. Then there was Paul Walker, quick and sharp and attentive.

For years I'd struggled with my weight more than anything else and it affected every bit of me: my energy, my creativity, my sexual activity. Being morbidly obese and all that went with it – waddling instead of walking, practically having to roll out of bed to get up – was horrible. I felt as if my weight was the key to everything in my life. I'd got so fat and ugly I really couldn't stand the sight of myself any more. I had a dread of going to awards ceremonies, thinking if I had to go up on stage and thread my way through all those tables, the size I was, I didn't know if I'd actually manage it. I didn't want to go to see Liverpool play at Anfield and be worried I'd get stuck in the turnstile going into the ground. That's how bad it was. I had to do something drastic.

Going to Egypt in 2008 was my epiphany.

22

I knew I was depressed because I was desperate for a holiday. Whenever I feel low I have a need to escape, go far from home. I suppose in my head it's about leaving all the day-to-day stuff behind, properly out of sight for a bit, and getting away from whatever it is that's dragging me down. That's the idea, anyway. It doesn't always work. Often, whatever it is that's preying on my mind comes with me.

Before I went to Egypt in 2008, my life was a mess and my self-esteem was so low I couldn't shut off the voice inside my head that said, 'No wonder, you deserve it.' My love life was a disaster, I was homeless, staying at my mum's, wondering how I'd managed to mess things up so much that at the age of forty-five I didn't even have a place of my own. I was earning good money in *Shameless* but I wasn't managing it. I'd never budgeted or saved. It was as if I wasn't capable. I was doing idiotic things, like lending someone money to have a holiday or buy their fella a present when my rent was due. When people talk of being generous to a fault, I truly was. My behaviour was completely irresponsible. Being bipolar, going from one extreme to another, didn't help. One month I'd have £60,000 in the bank, the next I'd have sixty pence.

All that paled into insignificance compared with being so fat. That was what was really depressing me. I was huge. There was no mystery about it. I was eating too much, eating the wrong things. I ate and ate and ate, using food as a crutch in the same way I had alcohol. Being big made me miserable, so then I'd eat even more. I had become a greedy fat bastard doing all the things greedy fat bastards do. I'd order a huge pizza and pretend there was somebody else with me when the pizza man came to the door. I'd have four or five bars of chocolate hidden under the duvet when I went to bed and stuff my face. I would eat six bags of crisps in a row. It wasn't as if I enjoyed eating. There was no pleasure in it any more. Food had become an obsession, a compulsion. I was gorging on rubbish, shovelling it in until I was so full I couldn't eat another thing. I'd binge and hate myself afterwards for my greed, my lack of control. The amount I was eating was making me feel sick. The problem was I couldn't stop.

On holiday in Egypt I reached breaking point.

Almost as soon as we arrived in Sharm El Sheikh I didn't feel right. I couldn't quite put my finger on it. We got ready and went for dinner. The others – Dannielle, her best friend, Baby Lee, my niece Michaela and my friend Richie – were in high spirits, excited about being away, babbling on about getting a tan, going on trips, having a good time. I wasn't quite with it. We'd had one of those horrible, bumpy flights, the plane lurching and dropping like a stone as we went through turbulence, and my stomach had been upset, so maybe that was all it was. I was conscious, too, that playing Mimi meant I no longer had anonymity. The show was getting bigger. In 2008, we were doing sixteen episodes, twice as many as the year before. The growing popularity of *Shameless* meant wherever I went, I was recognized; not that I minded in the least. Having my profile raised thanks to Mimi and being in such a brilliant series was truly a dream come true. It made me incredibly proud. I'd had people come up to me at the airport in Manchester and now there were other British holiday-makers wanting to say hello and have pictures taken. Everyone was nice, saying how much they loved the show. It had never been a problem meeting fans of *Shameless*, but all of a sudden, out of the blue, I had a sense of being horribly exposed. I can't even explain it. My head was all over the place. Over dinner, it began to play on my mind that every-where I went and everything I did would be scrutinized. It was crazy. I'd never felt that way before.

As I've said, I'm the kind of person who really doesn't care what other people think. I've always been like that. Don't get me wrong, I'm not oblivious. Being fat, I was conscious of being judged and disapproved of, and was well aware of how some people looked at me, as if I was disgusting. I'd always told myself what mattered was how I felt inside – but the truth was I felt like shit. I was deeply unhappy about my weight, hated how I looked, and it was starting to overwhelm me.

While Dannielle and the others chatted away over dinner, making plans, I wasn't listening. My mind was elsewhere. I felt a familiar flutter of panic in my chest and tried to ignore it. It wouldn't go away. I told myself that maybe all I needed was a good night's sleep. I couldn't have been more wrong.

In my room, I unpacked the rest of my things. I'd bought new stuff for the holiday – sandals, floaty kaftans, lovely things. Looking at them, I couldn't see why I'd bothered. Everything struck me as shapeless and baggy, unflattering. Whatever I wore, I was still going to be fat. I stood in front of the mirror and held up a sun dress, trying to picture myself in it. My eyes filled with tears. I knew I'd never wear it.

After the first day, I refused to leave the room. The others brought toast and a boiled egg back from breakfast for me. They were heading off to spend the day riding quad bikes and wanted me to go. In the past, I'd always been the person at the fun fair who held the coats while everyone else went on the rides, the fatty waving at the rollercoaster as it thundered past. It had never bothered me. I guess that's what they were expecting, that I'd go and watch while they tore across the desert. I said I wasn't going. They did what they could to talk me round, but I wasn't having it. I actually wanted them to stay with me, which was totally irrational.

In the end, they went off and left me. I spent the day in my room with the curtains closed, watching garbage on TV. Outside, it was 30-odd degrees, glorious. I lay on the bed in my leggings and fleece, air-conditioning blasting away. The whole time they were gone I was worried sick. What if one of them fell off? You heard terrible things about the bikes being unsafe, the lack of any regulation. I fretted, imagining all sorts, Dannielle and them racing about, doing daft things, none of them wearing helmets. Hours went by and I got myself really worked up. As soon as they came back, full of

it, saying what a ball they'd had, not a scratch on them, I
went mad.

'I've been on my own *all day*!'

'You should have come with us.'

'Stuck in this *fucking room* watching telly—'

'Nobody made you!'

'I asked you not to go. Would it have killed you to keep me
company?'

'We're *on holiday*! What was stopping you coming with us?'

'I DIDN'T WANT TO COME!'

'STOP MOANING, THEN!'

We had a huge bust-up, proper screaming and shouting.

I knew I was being unfair, totally unreasonable, but I
couldn't help it.

When they went for dinner I stayed in the room. For the
rest of the holiday, the days settled into a pattern. The others
would go for breakfast, bring me something back, head out
for the day, come back full of what they'd been doing, shower
and change for dinner, come back again about ten-thirty,
ready to go clubbing. In the early hours, Michaela would
creep in and get into bed. Usually, I pretended to be asleep.
While they made the most of their holiday, I never left the
room. I couldn't. I lay on the bed with the curtains shut, TV
on, feeling frantic, not knowing what the hell was wrong with
me, getting by on crisps and tortillas and toast and bottles of
water.

I'd lost the plot and it terrified me. I was in no fit state to
explain to the others what was going on; I expected them to
work it out, somehow. My moods were erratic. One minute
I'd be saying I didn't want them to go out, begging them to

stay with me; the next I'd be telling them to fuck off. Sheer madness.

It was hard for Dannielle because she'd had to live with my mania and depression and a lot more besides when she was young. I don't think she ever really understood what it was about. We had some terrible rows in Egypt, murder. She would come in pissed and angry and tell me to get a grip. As far as she was concerned, I was being selfish, spoiling things. I thought she was being a little bitch. When Richie wouldn't stick up for me, I got upset with him as well. Baby Lee and our Michaela, bless her, kept out of it. I didn't know how to explain in a way they would understand that I was experiencing the most crushing depression, barely functioning, and needed help. Instead, I got angry and defensive and ripped into them. It was completely unreasonable. If I didn't know what the fuck was going on, how could anyone else be expected to? For five days I stayed shut away in my hotel room, falling apart, feeling hurt and angry and abandoned. It was as if I'd spent my life fixing other people, and when it came to it no one knew how the fuck to fix me. On the plane home, I wasn't in the mood to speak to any of them.

We landed at Manchester Airport and I went straight to my mum's and broke down. It all came flooding out. I was miserable, falling out with everybody. It was nuts. At the root of it all, I hated being fat, and nobody was to blame but me. My obesity was my own fault – not the bullies in the playground or the stress of having a child on my own or my depression or my dad dying five years before … It was *me* who'd let myself get like that and I was filled with self-hate, not just for how I looked, but because I couldn't control it or do a thing about it. I had run out of ideas. All the dieting over the years had got me nowhere. With my drinking, the only way I'd managed to get on top of it was by abstaining from alcohol. I couldn't abstain from food. I was in absolute despair.

I told my mum how I felt and she came up with the idea of trying a gastric balloon. She could be a funny article, my mother, but whenever I needed her she was there. We rang round three clinics and found out about the procedure. Right then, it seemed my only chance of getting my eating under control. The people at the Hospital Group were the nicest on the phone, so I decided to go with them. God bless her, my mum stumped up the £5,000 to pay for it and I was booked in to have it done two days later, on 17 March 2008.

The night before I went in to have the balloon fitted, I'd booked a cab to take me to Manchester at seven the next morning. Mum was working, doing a night shift as a carer, and I was on my own, under strict instructions from the clinic not to have anything to eat after midnight. Before the deadline, I went and had a look in the fridge and rummaged in the kitchen cupboards. I wasn't even hungry but I had a compulsion to eat, any old rubbish I could get my hands on. I found a Fray Bentos steak pie and put it in the oven, peeled a load of potatoes and mashed them with a big lump of butter, and then I sat and ate the lot – kept going even when I knew I'd had enough. Afterwards, I felt violently ill. I was enormous, absolutely enormous, and I thought, 'This has to stop or I'm going to die, and if I don't die I'm going to kill myself.'

The next day I was at the clinic in Manchester, retching as

the balloon was passed down my throat and into my stomach, where it was inflated with saline. The idea of the balloon is that you feel full and can't eat the way you did before. It's a short procedure, about fifteen minutes, done under sedation, but I found it traumatic. It was like having some kind of alien inside me, moving around, and it made me feel really sick. I was due to stay in hospital overnight and then come home but I was so ill, not even able to keep water down, that it was five days before I was discharged. I was on a drip, rolling around the bed, moaning in agony. Understandably, the surgeon was anxious. He watched me retching and throwing up and suffering excruciating cramps, and wanted to take the balloon out. Not everyone can tolerate it and I was presenting all the classic symptoms of rejection. Whenever he broached the subject of removing it, I said no, to give it one more day. 'I'm fine,' I said, in between bouts of sickness. For me, it was a lifeline, a chance to start shifting the weight, and that was all I cared about. It would have to come out after six months anyway, which didn't seem that long to put up with feeling lousy. No matter how bad I felt, I was determined to stick with it.

Once I got home, I was on liquids. In theory, anyway. In reality, I could barely manage anything. What I did get down came back up again. Some days, I was so sick I'd end up sitting in the bath, sobbing. My mum would come in to see how I was doing.

'Do you want anything to eat, Chris? I can do some porridge.'

I'd shake my head, feeling like death, battling the urge to throw up for the umpteenth time. At least the weight was coming off. Within a couple of weeks I'd lost 18 pounds.

'You look great, by the way,' Mum said.

When my mother offered to put up the money for my gastric balloon, I don't suppose she thought for one second it would make me so ill that she'd be cleaning up after me day in, day out. I was sick as a dog. Everywhere. Vomiting became a way of life. If I went out it would have to be somewhere where the toilets were close by in case I needed to make a dash. Back at work on *Shameless*, everyone knew about the balloon, mainly because I never stopped talking about it. I was constantly throwing up and learning to live with it. Most of the time, there was no warning. I'd experience a sudden wave of nausea and seconds later I was heaving. In the minibus heading back to the hotel after a day on set with Sean Gilder and a couple of the others, someone would go, 'You look a bit green . . . ' Next thing I'd be yelling to stop the bus so I could hang out the door and be sick on the hard shoulder. After it happened a few times, no one batted an eyelid.

We used to stay at what was then the Mint Hotel in the centre of Manchester, where the staff always went out of their way to be good to us. One night I was about to check in, chatting away to the girl at reception, Sean with me and Alice Barry, who played Lillian. I seem to remember Karen Bryson, Avril in the show, being there too. There was all the usual milling about you'd expect in a busy hotel and, without warning, I was sick. All over the desk, the floor, the sign welcoming you to the Mint . . . I couldn't do a thing about it. A split second after feeling rough I was vomiting. The hotel staff were wonderful, insisting it was fine and not to worry, but I felt terrible. It was horrendous.

When I wasn't being sick – which was hardly ever – I could only manage tiny amounts of food. As time wore on, the nauseous feeling eased a bit, although it never really went away. I could see why some people just couldn't stick with having a gastric balloon, but I was willing to put up with it, however much discomfort I felt, because I was losing weight, and within a few weeks I could see a real difference. That was a good enough incentive for me.

I'd been back from Egypt about six weeks when I went to the gym and bumped into Richie. I hadn't spoken to him since the holiday.

'I can't apologize for the way I was,' I said. 'I couldn't help it. I was having a breakdown.'

'I know. I just didn't know what to do about it,' he said.

Richie and I had met about five years earlier when DSTM, the company I had with Dean Sullivan, was up and running, and he was my PA for a while. I adored him and he was a grafter, but he was always late. *Always*. It drove me mad. In the end, we agreed the whole PA thing wasn't working and parted company, but by then, he'd become a good friend, someone I could call on any hour of the day or night. Over the years, he had seen me in some terrible states with my depression.

The year before the Egypt trip, we'd been away to Tunisia, another five-star resort, and I'd had an almighty meltdown. One of my drama students, June Stenson, and her daughter, Penny, were with us. June was another incredible friend, kind and generous. If all she had was two slices of bread, she'd give you them.

A few days into the holiday I had the tantrum to end all tantrums.

One of the pool guys at the hotel had taken a shine to Penny and wouldn't go away. He was smarmy, a proper pest, that bit too full of himself, and I didn't like him at all. We were in the restaurant one day, the place packed for afternoon tea, and, as usual, the pool guy was all over us, smarming away. When he grabbed hold of my wrist to look at my watch, I saw red. I don't like anyone grabbing me, especially not some sleazy guy I don't even know.

I grabbed hold of his wrist. 'How do you like it?' I said.

He gave me what he probably thought was a playful slap on the arm – *big* mistake – and I smacked him across the face. I still don't think he understood what he was dealing with because he got me in a bear hug and held on tight. I screamed and swore and struggled while he hung on, smiling his smarmy smile, which made me about a hundred times more furious. He seemed to think it was funny, that we were playing, having a laugh. *Very* fucking big mistake. When he started laughing, I lost it, and as soon as he loosened his grip I went for him. Richie and June had to drag me off.

By then I was livid. I stormed through the busy restaurant to the buffet table, which was laden with lovely cakes and pastries and crepes, all set out on huge silver platters. Around me, people were enjoying their afternoon tea, and on the other side of the room was the pool guy, still with an inane grin on his stupid face. Richie and June were frozen to the spot. I picked up a platter in each hand and hurled them across the room. They clattered off the tiled floor, cakes and crepes going everywhere. I hit loads of people. About the only person I didn't get was the one I was aiming at, the pool guy. A bald chap in a smart white shirt and casual pants standing at the tea urn ended up with two crepes stuck to his head. He made no attempt to remove them, just carried on pouring hot water into cups as if nothing had happened. Everyone looked the other way. It had gone very quiet. I hurled another stream of abuse at the pool guy, who was ashen, then I spun around and marched out of the restaurant. The place had been done out to give it the look of a luxurious desert tent with swathes of silk fabric hanging from the ceiling. As I thundered underneath them, I reached up and yanked the whole lot down, leaving a trail of destruction in my wake. I flung open the door, gave it such a slam I'm surprised it stayed on its hinges, and ran to the toilets where I sank to the floor and wailed. June came and found me and took me upstairs.

Thinking about it, from Richie's point of view, what happened in Egypt probably wasn't so bad.

23

Once the gastric balloon came out after six months, I liked what I saw when I looked in the mirror. I'd lost more than 4 stone and had gone from wearing a size 28 to a size 20. I was still fat, but I felt happier and healthier than I had in a long time. The problem was, with the balloon gone there was nothing to stop me going back to my old overeating ways.

Towards the end of 2008, I went to Las Vegas with my mum and Dannielle. We stayed at the Bellagio Hotel, which was amazing. I spent a fortune on shows and limousines and champagne for the others and ... eating out. The food was fantastic and the portions were what you'd call generous, as you'd expect in the States. I was back to my old ways, having restaurant meals every day, eating way too much. A lot of it was healthy stuff, like lobster, but in ridiculous quantities. Vegas was hot and I got through a ton of ice cream. All the weight I'd lost began to go back on. There's a photo of me with my mum and Dannielle queuing up for a ride on a gondola and I look about twenty years older than I do now. Dannielle was big too. The look on the poor fella's face when he saw us getting into his boat was priceless. He must have thought he'd never get it moving.

I've always been in a relationship of one sort or another – I've never been single for long. There have been some good relationships, some bad ones; sometimes I've had my heart broken, sometimes I've been the heartbreaker. That's just the way it goes. When Channel 4 asked me to do *Celebrity Big Brother* in 2009, I was just coming out of one of the bad ones – a complicated relationship that had been messing with my head for a while. I jumped at the opportunity – I saw it as my chance to escape the madness of my real life for a while.

In the run-up to *CBB*, I was feeling insecure, paranoid, desperate, lonely, angry, defensive, unhappy, depressed . . . fat. Even though I had regular work and money coming in, my finances were still all over the place. I was spending huge amounts with not much idea where it was all going. Thinking about it, holidays took chunks out of my bank balance. The Vegas trip had cost thousands.

The one good thing in my life was *Shameless*. The series was getting bigger and better, with another sixteen episodes planned for 2009. Once we got cracking, I knew I'd be back in a work routine that was full on, and I couldn't wait. My career was the one area in my life where I truly felt I was in control. Outside of work, I had no control whatsoever – over my size, my relationship, my money. I was a mess, mentally and physically.

I had no doubts about doing *Big Brother*; the money was good and I was up for the experience. I also thought there would be a limited supply of food so I might even lose weight!

Only a couple of people knew I was doing *CBB*. I kept it really quiet. The only niggle I had about going in was how my mum and Dannielle would react. The pair of them were obsessed with *Big Brother* and I knew they'd be watching. God in heaven, they'd hit the roof when they saw me appear on the launch show. Before the show, I did all the profile interviews and psychological assessments and was deemed fit to take part. I was due to travel to London on 1 January, so I made up some story about going to a New Year's Eve party in LA, then checked into the Mint Hotel in Manchester with my friend Darren Johnson. He took me to the station the next morning and I got the train to Euston. The funny thing was, I spotted Terry Christian boarding the same train as me, a few carriages up, and guessed he too was on his way to *CBB*. I thought it best to keep a low profile, since you're not supposed to know who your fellow housemates are. In London, as soon as I got off the train, a voice said, 'Tina Malone!' Terry had spotted me. 'Are you going into *Big Brother*, then?' I told him I was, that I'd been trying to avoid bumping into him. It turned out he was supposed to be on a later train but had set off early. We had a chat and left the station separately, Terry going one way, me heading in the opposite direction.

As you'd expect, the whole *CBB* experience is cloak and dagger. The level of secrecy is phenomenal. At Euston, a blacked-out car picked me up. On the back seat was a pair of headphones and a towel. As we drove through London, I had no idea where we were going, just that I was spending the night in a hotel somewhere. As we got close to wherever we were going, the driver told me to put on the headphones and cover my head with the towel. The car slowed to a stop and I felt the door open. Someone helped me out and guided me through what felt like some kind of underground corridor to a lift. We got in and went up to what must have been a sealed-off corridor, where they let me take off the headphones and the thing on my head. I was given the code name Lilac.

I had minders posted outside my door and a chaperone inside the room. She was with me the whole time. She went through the contents of my suitcase, took all my stuff out, and covered the labels on my shampoo and make-up and what-have-you with duct tape. The producers came to talk to me and I had visits from the doctor and psychiatrist. Every time there was a knock on the door, I was ushered into the bathroom while the chaperone checked to see who was there. If I wanted a cigarette, the chaperone checked to make sure none of the other houseguests were out in the smoking area before taking me outside. It was all, 'Lilac wants to go out. Can I confirm Scarlet is back in her room?' I couldn't tell you anything about where I was, because every time I ventured out for a fag, the headphones and towel went back on. It was surreal.

The next day, it was the same rigmarole with the towel, the headphones and the car with blacked-out windows on the way to the studio. I spent hours with the chaperone in my dressing room, had more visits from the producers and psychiatrist, then it was back into the car, which drove off somewhere. I'd been told to stay covered up until I got instructions via the headphones to step out of the car. All the weird stuff that goes on during the build-up to *Big Brother*, when they keep you quite literally in the dark, makes it feel insane. Your thought processes go into overdrive and the tension whips you into a weird frame of mind where you end up thinking, 'What am I doing? Am I off my cake?' And that's before you even set foot inside the house. I must have sat in silence for half an hour or so, no idea what was going on, before a voice spoke to me through the headphones.

'Tina, get out of the car.'

As soon as I took the headphones off, I could hear screaming. It was deafening. The door of the car opened and I got out and stepped forward on to a red carpet and into bright studio lights. Davina McCall was in front of me, hundreds of people yelling, going mental. It was terrifying. I've no idea how my legs carried me forward or what I said for those few seconds I spent chatting with Davina before going into the house. The whole thing was a blur. I stepped inside and the first person I saw was LaToya Jackson, which freaked me out even more. It really was the most bizarre experience.

In Liverpool, my mum and Dannielle had settled down together to watch *CBB*. As far as they knew, I was in LA. The first six housemates went in and then my name was announced and there I was, larger than life, waving, beaming away. Oh. My. God. I can only imagine the looks on their faces. My mum told me later it was such a shock seeing me she almost passed out. Dannielle absolutely hated me being in there. It was one thing a bunch of strangers showing themselves up,

In costume as Mimi Maguire with *Shameless* writer Paul Abbott, David Threlfall (Frank Gallagher), Annabelle Apsion (Monica Gallagher) and other members of the cast, opening the new purpose-built set in 2007. I was at my largest then, and remember being really uncomfortable that day.

On set with David in 2009. As an actor and director, he brought out the best in me.

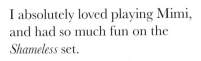

I absolutely loved playing Mimi, and had so much fun on the *Shameless* set.

Entering the *Celebrity Big Brother* house in January 2009. I didn't know what I was letting myself in for!

My explosive argument with Coolio made all the front pages, but I was happy to kiss and make up by the time it came to leave the house.

At the *Celebrity Big Brother* wrap party, with my mum and Dannielle.

L–R: Doreen, Carol, me, mum and Lynn. My family mean more to me than anything in the world.

I met former solider Paul Chase at a fitness boot camp after *Big Brother*, in 2009. It wasn't quite love at first sight, but it didn't take long for me to realise he was the one.

At our engagement party in 2010, with my nieces Michaela and Bobbie, my mum, me, my *Shameless* castmate Ben Batt, and Paul.

With my beautiful bridesmaids on our wedding day, in August 2010. L-R: Casey, Michaela, Bobbie and Alex.

Meeting my wonderful husband-to-be at the altar.

This photo says it all. Marrying Paul was one of the happiest days of my life.

With my best mate in the world, Kerry Williams.

Me and Paul in our glad rags at the 2011 National Television Awards.

On the *This Morning* sofa in January 2012, showing off my new slim figure.

Paul and I revealing that we are expecting a baby on *This Morning*, in May 2013.

Me, Paul and the bump.
September 2013.

An emotional new dad and baby Flame in hospital, 15 December 2013.

Proud big sister Dannielle gives Flame a feed!

Me, Paul and our beautiful Flame – the best Christmas present ever!

another when the woman slobbing about in the dressing gown and biting her toenails was her mother.

I had a great time in the house. It was crazy. Straight away, I warmed to LaToya Jackson and got friendly with Ulrika Jonsson, a real woman's woman, and Mutya Buena, one of the Sugababes. She was lovely and we became close. I wasn't sure I'd click with the glamour model, Lucy Pinder, but she was intelligent and smart and beautiful and we got along fine. The other housemates were Michelle Heaton from the pop group Liberty X, Ben Adams, who'd been in a boy band, the politician Tommy Sheridan, the actor Verne Troyer, Coolio, the rapper, and, of course, Terry Christian. No surprises there.

I can't say I forgot the cameras were on us the whole time, but I wasn't bothered since that was what I'd signed up for. One of the toughest aspects of being in the house was not being able to get away from other people. Every room you went into somebody was already there, so there was no 'me' time. There was no TV, no pens, no paper, and, as someone who makes lists every day of my life, that was hard. I've got a racing mind, so I was first up and last to bed every day. I didn't find the experience boring, not in the slightest, and I enjoyed the tasks. They had me dressed up as a fairy doing daft stuff and I loved that. I wasn't so keen on the game where you were asked questions and if you gave the wrong answer you got an electric shock. They really hurt.

LaToya and I ended up talking a lot, and she really opened up to me.

'You know, we have a lot in common,' she said at one point. That made me smile. Yeah, right. LaToya had grown up with fame, privilege, success, in one of the most high-profile families in the world, whereas I . . . hadn't. I found her warm and kind and quirky, although at times I felt she might as well have been from another planet, her experience of life was so different. The day I made a roast dinner I got her helping out, chopping vegetables. It was all new to her. I suppose in the world of the Jacksons something as mundane as cooking was an alien concept. I got the impression the kitchen wasn't a part of the house she was all that familiar with. I was peeling potatoes and she stood slicing carrots, saying, 'I've never done this before.'

I had to laugh. 'Don't worry, love, you'll be on the onions in a minute. That's a whole new experience.'

The only person I had a problem with in the house was the rapper, Coolio. He was full of, 'I'm a gangster, I'm a *g*,' which got on my nerves. 'If you're a *g*, I'm a fucking *Vogue* model,' I said. He bragged about losing his virginity at the age of twelve to a girl of fourteen and went on about being a bully at school and how no one dared stand up to him. When he cut out the bullshit, he was actually harmless, but we clashed more than once. He was acting like a bully, being vile to Ulrika, coming on to Mutya, a girl half his age who was not the slightest bit interested. She was so polite, not wanting to offend him, but it was obvious to everyone she didn't want to know. When he wouldn't take the hint, I told him to leave her alone.

'You're a man in your forties, you've had about ten wives, you've got about ten kids, and Mutya's a young girl. You don't mean jack-shit to her, so leave her alone.' I couldn't believe that a man of his age was picking on a young girl.

He didn't like it one little bit and told me to shut my mouth. Well, I wasn't having any of that. I went ballistic, yelling at him that as he didn't pay my bills or sleep with me, he had no right to tell me to shut up. I told him some home truths, and all he could respond was, 'Shut the fuck up!'.

They only showed half of it on TV. The newspapers went mad. 'Coolio gets another warning after aggressive bust-up with Tina Malone'. 'Coolio lands Channel 4 in new "bully" row'.

The worst moment for me was when I got my letter from home. It's a strange thing being so cut off from everything, in a little cocoon, with no idea what's going on in the world outside or how it must be for your friends and family watching you on screen. All the others got lovely letters from home. Reading them out was one of the most emotional parts of the whole experience. 'We're so proud of you. We love you. We miss you, you're doing really great.' All the letters were so touching, they had everybody crying buckets.

When it was my turn and I was told my letter was from my mum and Dannielle, I started to get anxious. I guessed it wouldn't be anything like the others. It said, 'Chris, stop swearing, you're embarrassing yourself. We'll see you soon.' That was it. Not the slightest bit of encouragement, no mention of them missing me, nothing to say they loved me. I was absolutely gutted. *You're embarrassing yourself.* Everyone in the room went quiet. Right then, if the ground had opened up and swallowed me, it would have been a relief. I was hurt, horribly humiliated. At the same time, I wasn't surprised. I love my mother to death and my daughter comes before anything and everything in my life, but I've always had a difficult relationship with the pair of them. I don't know why, exactly. Saying that, I know I've never been easy. Me and my mum argued a lot, always, and she used to say, 'The trouble is, Chris, I know you better than you know yourself.' She thought I could be nasty, she didn't like bad language in any shape or form, and she felt you should never embarrass yourself in life or on TV – so me being in *Shameless* can't have been easy for her. I was the kind of person who did what the hell I wanted to do. I suppose she saw me as a loose cannon. With Dannielle, I poured love and attention and confidence on her, absolutely devoured her, yet as she grew up I felt she pulled away from me. Now, I can see she found my fame difficult, and that's something I've only really taken on board in the last twelve months or so.

Once I came out of the house, I asked my manager, David Samuel, why he hadn't got one of my friends to write the letter, say something nice. I got on well with David. He handled my work commitments – reality TV appearances and so on – aside from acting roles, and I knew I could count on him to do what was best for me. The business with the letter was out of his hands, apparently. It had to be my next of kin. I tried talking to my mum and Dannielle, asked them what on earth they were thinking, but they had no idea why I was so upset. Under normal circumstances, what goes on between us – all the tricky stuff – stays under wraps. There was no hiding the *CBB* letter, though. I couldn't help thinking those few lines revealed so much about them and how they felt about me.

There's a lot of stress and emotional bullshit that goes on in a bipolar's head. On the mantelpiece at home I've got a John Lennon quotation that a friend gave me. It reads: 'Part of me suspects that I'm a loser and the other part thinks that I'm God Almighty.'

I totally relate to that.

When I'm low and skint and depressed, I can get really down. What goes on in my head is something like, 'God, I was fat for twenty years. I'm a shit mother or I'd have done it the right way and brought my daughter up somewhere better than in a bedsit, struggling. I'm neurotic and Dannielle saw me being eccentric and bipolar, having mood swings, drinking and so on. I've never been a great daughter or a great sister because I'm cranky and moody and nasty and volatile . . . blah, blah, blah.'

When I'm feeling good, the God Almighty side kicks in, and I'll go: 'Actually, no, I was obsessed with my daughter, gave her everything I could and she never went without. I spent time with her – reading, watching films, going places. I built my life round her at the same time I was trying to run my career, and we were happy. She meant more to me than any man ever could and every man I went with, from gangster to copper, was made fully aware of it from day one. My little brother: I took him everywhere, gave him everything, and supported and encouraged him, and I can't have been all that bad a daughter because I made my parents laugh and did what my dad drummed into me and achieved success as an actor.'

Up and down, on and on – that's me.

The *CBB* letter really got under my skin and triggered stuff that was never far from the surface and had a tendency to gnaw away – like my daughter never watching me in *Shameless*, not even my fat episode. I felt like all my life I'd been vying for approval and not quite getting it. Not from my mum and dad and Dannielle, anyway. Growing up, I was always desperate for my parents to give me a bit of praise, tell me I looked nice and what-have-you. When I started acting and they came to see me on stage, what I wanted to hear most was them say they were proud of me. All the good reviews in the world, other people telling me I was talented or funny or clever, meant nothing when I never heard it from my mum and dad.

As time went on and I was doing well, I pulled out the stops to impress them. The panto in Stoke-on-Trent in 1995 was a good example. For the opening night, my dad was coming from Liverpool with my old school friend Karen Maloney's parents, Irene and Vince, and I wanted it to be really special. I laid on champagne, a chauffeur-driven gold Rolls-Royce Phantom for them, and booked them into the Holiday Inn, where Mum and Dannielle were also staying. Karen's folks were blown away, going on non-stop about how amazing everything was, that they'd felt like film stars in the Roller. My dad made some comment about the engine being nice and smooth and that was about it. If he was impressed, you'd never have known.

I took my mum and Dannielle on loads of holidays. As well as the Vegas trip, I took Mum to Ibiza and Cyprus, Dannielle to Spain and New York and San Francisco. I even paid for them to go on holiday to Jamaica without me because I couldn't get time off work. At times I wanted to scream. All I wanted was some appreciation. *Something.* Thanks for the champagne, the hotel suite. You look lovely. And, by the way, you were great on stage tonight.

It didn't seem too much to ask.

I was voted out of the *Big Brother* house after fifteen days. As soon as I came out, I was whipped away to a room for a chat with two psychiatrists. They had some treats for me: a mint Aero, a packet of cheese-and-onion crisps, and a diet Coke – all my favourite things, basically – which was a nice touch. From there, I went on set to do an interview with Davina. While all this was going on, Mutya had decided she didn't want to stay in the house without me and had left too. It was quite a night. Nobody could understand why I'd signed up for *CBB* in the first place. It wasn't as if I was at a loose end. I had a job. In another few weeks I'd be back on *Shameless*, doing twelve-hour days, working on the new series. I told Davina I'd done it for the big fat cheque, which was true. It was hard to turn down £120,000. What I didn't say was that it was about much more than the money, that the house represented a place where I could take a break, take stock of my life. When I came out I knew for sure that I wanted out of my unhealthy relationship. For good.

24

I've got a picture I carry round with me from when I was in the *Celebrity Big Brother* house in early 2009 and I look like a beached whale. Emotionally, though, I was in a good place after *CBB*. I was single, I had money in the bank, I'd had my teeth done – a set of cosmetic veneers, which looked amazing – and I'd made up my mind I was going to have a gastric band fitted. I went on holiday to Jamaica, took my friend Jeanette for her fortieth, and her sister, Christine, as well as Michaela, my niece, for her twenty-first. Mrs Money Bags. I was in great spirits, full of my own pizzazz, when my manager, David Samuel, signed me up for a week at a boot camp in the Peak District. I didn't much fancy it, but he talked me round. 'Look, it's a couple of grand and if you really hate it you can leave,' he said. Reluctantly, I agreed, having no idea what I was letting myself in for, never dreaming those few days would change my life for ever.

I arranged to take our Michaela with me. The night before we were due to go, I almost backed out. I was knackered after a nightmare five-and-a-half-hour journey home from a wedding in Dorset, and boot camp was the last thing I felt like. In all honesty, I was beginning to wish I'd never agreed to do it in the first place.

I arrived looking like a fat trollop in a fleece and a beanie hat that did nothing for me. I had no eyelashes and my top lip could have done with waxing, not that I was bothered. I wasn't out to impress anyone. I'd packed an emergency stash of chocolate – mint Aero and Minstrels – and the first thing they did was empty my bag and rob my sweets to stop me cheating. I was devastated. At least Michaela and I had nice bedrooms while the other guests were in a dormitory. From the off, it was a strict regime. At six in the morning we'd be up and out on a two-and-a-quarter-mile run to warm up, all of us wearing orange vests with numbers on, like convicts. All day we worked in teams, building rafts, playing rounders, lifting, climbing, running, jumping ... you name it. I was always on the losing team. We'd finally knock off at around nine in the evening. It was horrendous, torture. I absolutely hated it. Michaela, twenty-one and fit as a fiddle, found it so gruelling she was throwing up. That tells you how tough it was. The morning after my first day, I woke up feeling as if I'd been battered all over. Every inch of my body ached. I couldn't face another day of star jumps and circuits, and was under the impression that, being a celebrity guest, I wouldn't have to do all the activities and could pick and choose. I decided to take things easy, opt out of some of the more strenuous stuff.

There were three trainers, ex-soldiers, one called Paul Chase. He came knocking on my door, telling me to get out and do the run or the tug-of-war or whatever it was. I was fuming, going, 'I don't have to do all that stuff,' and he was going, 'Yes, you do.' I couldn't get away with anything. If he thought I was dragging my heels, he'd be on my case making me do press-ups as punishment. No matter how much I objected, it made no difference; Paul wasn't in the slightest bit fazed.

He was doing my head in.

We were on a strict 'no carb, no dairy' regime. Sheer misery, in other words. The idea was if you stuck to the plan you were guaranteed to lose around 7 to 10 pounds in a week. You didn't have much choice, not when all treats were confiscated. Compared with what I was used to, it was starvation rations. Breakfast was a tiny bowl of porridge and a piece of apple. Not even a whole one. Around eleven in the morning, after hours of hard-core training, the reward would be an oat biscuit with a thin layer of paté. Lunch was something simple and healthy and low-calorie like fish with broccoli and tomatoes. Everything was plain, no butter or sauces to improve the flavour. Dinner might be a bowl of lentil soup. I was a big fatty, used to eating what I wanted, so I was starving.

On the third day I'd had enough and very nearly went home. I had aches in places I didn't even know existed. The lack of food was making me snappy. I made arrangements for someone to come and get me and packed my stuff. Michaela pleaded with me to stay. For reasons I could not understand, she was actually starting to enjoy it. 'You're over the worst,'

she said. 'Just stick it out until Friday and get your certificate.'
I can't have been thinking straight – lack of food, probably –
because I let her talk me round.

Paul was starting to grow on me. I quite liked the fact he
wouldn't give in to me, plus he was funny and made me laugh.

Towards the end of the week we faced our biggest chal-
lenge, an eight-mile run. That was always going to be a
stretch for me. In fact, I wasn't sure I'd manage it. All the
others went sprinting off uphill and I was the straggler at the
back. Before long, the rest of them had disappeared. Paul
stayed with me and kept me going. It took me almost seven
hours to complete the course and we chatted all the way. I
found out a bit about him, that he was from Birkenhead and
had been in the army for ten years, serving in Northern
Ireland and Iraq and Afghanistan. He was down to earth, not
in the least bit arsed about me being on telly, which made a
nice change. At the party on the final night I saw him dancing and it struck me that as well as being fit and funny and
interesting, he was also cute and sexy.

After boot camp, I went home to Manchester, where I was
staying with a friend, Jeanette, in Salford Quays, while I
looked for a place to rent. Paul and I were in touch, swapping
texts. The following weekend I was teaching drama in
Liverpool and we arranged to meet up for a drink afterwards.
Beyond that we'd made no plans, but things went so well we
ended up checking into the Atlantic Tower hotel and stayed
there, holed up in our room for the entire weekend. It was
wonderful, amazing. There were no awkward moments or
uncomfortable silences, nothing about him I didn't like. We
stayed indoors for two days, ordering room service, Paul

drinking champagne, me having hot chocolate, not getting out of bed, feeling totally debauched. For the first time in ages I felt I could be myself, that here was a man I didn't need to impress. It didn't matter to him what size I was because he fancied me anyway. I kept thinking there had to be a catch. There's always a catch. Isn't there? In the past, there had been. Not this time. We clicked on every level, and that was so rare in my experience.

When I got back to Manchester, Jeanette took one look at me and said, 'My God, you're really into this guy, aren't you?'

I was. Falling for Paul had thrown me completely. The last thing I had been looking for was a serious relationship. Since I'd ended things with my fella a few months earlier, I'd been dating three guys – a twenty-two-year-old, a thirty-year-old and a fifty-three-year-old – enjoying life, not taking anything too seriously. I hadn't banked on falling for someone I'd only just met.

I'd arranged to go to Nice in the south of France with my mum for a few days, and while I was away Paul and I kept in touch, texting and phoning. Every time I heard his voice, I had butterflies in my stomach. I hadn't felt like that about anyone for a very long time. The only thing that worried me was that, at forty-six, I was a lot older than him. He was coming up for twenty-seven, a year younger than Dannielle. I knew he'd had two long-term relationships before, both with young women, and would probably want to get married one day and have children.

Then again, so did I.

We made plans to meet up again at the weekend when I got back. He came over to Manchester and we went for something to eat. I could tell he was a bit distant, and when we got back to the apartment I asked him what was wrong. At boot camp, I'd told him about the guys I was seeing and joked about how I was enjoying my freedom and intended to mess around from then on, use and abuse, go for young guys with stamina. It was talk, my idea of a joke, but it seemed it had been preying on his mind. He was worried I saw him as the latest in a long line of dickheads.

It was as far from the truth as possible. I was dead serious and wanted him to know how I felt, so I asked if he'd like to move in with me. His jaw almost hit the floor. No wonder. We'd only known each other thirteen days. Actually, I was as surprised as he was. Until the words were out I hadn't known what I was going to say. I thought I should spell out what he was getting himself into if he said yes. I gave him one of my lists.

'Look, I'm not messing around,' I said. 'I'm a lot older than you, I'm bipolar, OCD, neurotic, opinionated, bombastic, arrogant, vain, insecure, deep, unconventional, driven, ambitious, self-obsessed. I sleep four or five hours a night, tops. If I want to get up at four in the morning and put a *Sopranos* DVD on or iron, or cook a roast dinner or a lemon drizzle cake, I'm going to do it.'

He looked at me.

I went on. 'I'm loud, selfish and needy at times, eccentric in every way. I'm also deeply romantic, loyal, honest, open and genuine. I want to get married, have a family, if possible. What I'm saying is I'm high-maintenance. Do you think you can all handle that?'

After a second or two, he said, 'Yeah, OK.'

He was meant to head off at teatime to get his stuff from home, but around two in the afternoon he decided to make a move and I thought that was it, I'd never see him again. *He thinks I'm a lunatic. I've totally blown it.* I needn't have worried. A few hours later he was back.

When I told Jeanette what I'd done, she thought I'd gone nuts. In the past, I'd tended to be wary and keep my relationships at arm's length. I'd never asked a man to move in with me. I hadn't even ever really lived with anybody, not properly. I'd move in for a few weeks, even a few months, but not with any real sense of it being for ever. It was nothing to do with not being serious or committed while I was involved – more that I'd always had a gut feeling that whoever I was seeing was not going to be for keeps. Even in the early stages of being with somebody, if you're really honest with yourself, I think you know whether or not it's right. You can feel it, inside.

I had made it a habit to travel light because it's easier to move on if all you have to pack is your toothbrush and a few clothes. Then I met Paul and I *knew*. We were compatible. He didn't want to change me. He had seen me at boot camp in a shapeless fleece and battered beanie hat, the moaning bastard at the back of the group, and didn't give two monkeys. He was warm and funny and *normal*. He was kind, bighearted. He was everything you'd want in a boyfriend.

The two of us could not have been more different. I'm a snob. I like academics and intellectuals, people who are well read, well travelled, like my dad. My world was TV and showbiz. Berkoff, Brecht, Shakespeare. What Paul knew was the army, conflict zones – Northern Ireland, Iraq, Afghanistan. It didn't matter in the slightest because we got on. Someone once said to me that if you have to work at a relationship, it's not right. It should flow.

We flowed.

We moved into a penthouse apartment at the Quays. Things had happened so quickly between us I hadn't had a chance to get to know his family, so I invited his mum and dad, Sue and Steve, and his younger brother, Shaun, over for dinner. I wanted everything to be perfect and decided to do roast chicken and steak and all the trimmings. I guessed his parents would have some concerns about the age difference and I wanted to reassure them. A list of shortcomings and neuroses like I'd given Paul probably wouldn't help. A relaxed meal might. Richie came over to give me a hand getting things ready and we sat up for hours the night before, polishing crystal glasses, peeling potatoes and parsnips, carrots and sprouts. I'd gone over the top, of course, and bought way too much food. There were enough sprouts for about twenty people. On the night, it all went to plan. The food was lovely and we got along fine. I think seeing Paul and I together put his parents' minds at rest. It was obvious how happy we were. Not the most conventional of relationships by some people's standards, maybe, but it worked, that much was obvious.

A few days later, we noticed a terrible smell in the apartment. We turned the place upside down trying to find out where it was coming from. I hadn't yet started back at *Shameless* and Paul and I were living the high life, eating out every night, having a great time. Coming home, we were almost being knocked out by the smell. It was as if there was a dead body in the place. We went through all the cupboards, checked under the sink, emptied the bin. Nothing. Every day it got worse. Finally, I opened the oven. The stench was so overpowering I almost passed out. On the middle shelf was a bowl of cooked sprouts, the ones left over from when Sue and Steve and Shaun had been for dinner the week before. They were in an advanced state of decomposition, absolutely disgusting. We bagged them up and put them out, but it was days before we managed to get rid of the smell.

Over the next few months we had a wonderful time. He met my friends and family, and everybody who knew me could see we were right together. We went to Vegas and stayed at the Venetian. When Stevie Wonder played the MEN Arena in Manchester we were there, twelve rows from the front, me sat between Paul and my mum, sobbing all the way through because the songs were ones I'd listened to with my dad. Paul came with me to the Royal Television Society Awards, the National Television Awards. It was all new to him, and it had to wreck his head a bit, being thrust into the limelight, rubbing shoulders with celebrities, doing the whole red-carpet thing. Very quickly, I realized he wasn't a bit fazed or impressed by any of it. He took it all in his stride, and I loved that.

Dannielle had left to go travelling in March 2009, a few weeks before I met Paul, and planned to be away for a year. Dannielle's trip was ambitious and she had a whole list of countries she wanted to see, including Vietnam, Thailand, Borneo, Sumatra, Australia and the States. Needless to say, I didn't want her to go. We'd never been apart for any length of time, and the thought of her thousands of miles away was hard to get to grips with. She was a few months off her twenty-eighth birthday, all grown-up, capable and independent, but she was still my little girl. The day I saw her off at the airport I was distraught, imagining all sorts. It turned out I was right to be concerned. She'd only been gone a few weeks when she was mugged and had her bag pinched in Vietnam. I was at work on *Shameless* when I got the call and was frantic, but she was OK, shaken up a bit, that was all. I'd have brought her home there and then if I could, but she wouldn't have it.

Every other day we spoke on the phone, so she knew about Paul. In August, I arranged for her to fly back from Melbourne so that she could meet him. Knowing how much Dannielle meant to me, Paul was understandably nervous. Actually, they got on fine, found the same things funny. It wasn't awkward at all. She could see I was happy. At the same time, she was wary. The age difference worried her. It probably felt weird that Paul was that bit younger than her and I think she was afraid he would leave me for some young girl half my age and I'd end up heartbroken. I don't think for one minute she thought it would last. She spent three nights with us and then she was off partying with her mates in Liverpool. In no time at all, we were back at the airport saying our goodbyes.

It was no easier letting her go than it had been a few months earlier, but at least I wasn't facing it on my own. I had Paul now. I also had a puppy, a little Teacup Yorkie, Bob. After Kelly, I'd sworn I would never have another dog because I knew how attached I'd get all over again, but ten years on, it felt like the right thing to do, and I got Bob the day before Dannielle left the previous March. He was like my little baby, a great source of comfort, while my daughter was away.

I was still huge and determined to lose weight. The year before, when I'd had the gastric balloon fitted, the surgeon had talked to me about going for a gastric band instead. It was a better option, in his opinion. At the time, I wouldn't consider it because it meant a general anaesthetic, and I was so enormous I really thought if they put me under I'd never wake up again. I had another irrational fear about the anaesthetic that stemmed from being a control freak. The idea of being helpless and at the mercy of other people made me anxious. I imagined being in the operating theatre and someone giving me a slap or lifting my top up and going, 'Look at the state of her!' When I tried explaining this to people, they looked at me as if I was off my cake. Finally, I decided to stop worrying and give the gastric band a go. Paul was a hundred per cent behind me, but never made me feel my weight was an issue for him. All he wanted was for me to be happy. Fat or thin, he would love me just the same, I knew that.

I was booked to go into hospital on 14 December 2009. The procedure had to be slotted in around my work commitments and Christmas was the only free time I had. Once the band was in place I wouldn't be able to eat solids for the next four to six weeks, so it was going to mean sitting down to a protein shake on Christmas Day. To me, that was a small price to pay. Three weeks before the op, I cut out the fags. With ten days to go, I went on to a pre-op diet of shakes and milk, ready for surgery.

I'd been busy on *Shameless*, doing a lot of exterior scenes, and the weather had been bad, freezing. I'd always felt the cold, but that winter seemed particularly harsh, and on drama shoots there's always a lot of hanging about in between scenes. You can be on set, outside, freezing your bits off for hours. In 2005, when I did a few days on the BBC period drama *Fingersmith*, on location in Kent, I was so cold I was almost in tears. Everybody else was OK and I wondered if I had Raynaud's, a condition that affects the blood supply, usually to your fingers and toes, and gets triggered by being cold or stressed. On *Shameless*, the wardrobe people, Ali, Lisa, Danielle and Bessie, kept me swathed in wraps and coats and packed my pockets with hand warmers, which should have been enough to keep me reasonably warm, but underneath the layers I was chilled to the bone. I remember doing a scene with Aaron McCusker and Ciaran Griffiths, who played Mimi's sons, Jamie and Micky, Laurence Till directing, as we loaded dodgy gear into the boot of a car. I was in thin leggings and shaking so much I could actually see it on camera. Sally Carman, who played Kelly the prostitute and was three stone wet through, out in all weathers in skimpy little dresses, was absolutely fine. God only knows how on earth she did it.

My mum could never understand why I suffered so much with the cold. 'Look at the size of you. How can you be cold when you're that fat?' she said.

I was indignant. 'I'm not a whale, you know! It's not blubber!'

On the morning of the gastric-band procedure, Paul and I drove to the private Dolan Park Hospital, near Birmingham. I was in the care of the Hospital Group again. As I got into my gown, ready for theatre, I was absolutely terrified. The anaesthetist came in and examined me and then my surgeon appeared with some bad news. There was a touch of pneumonia on my lungs, apparently, and they couldn't risk putting me under. The operation was going to have to wait. The possibility of it being postponed at the last minute had never crossed my mind. There was nothing for it other than to get dressed and go home. It would be months before I'd get another chance to have it done.

25

Paul and I had talked about getting married and he was saving up for an engagement ring. I was convinced he was going to propose on Christmas Day, 2009. I planned things so it would be romantic, just the two of us, and went all out to make sure it was the best Christmas either of us had ever had. We had eggs Benedict for breakfast and cracked open the champagne for Paul first thing. Paul is a simple soul, happy with very little, and if I'd bought him a pack of three vests for a tenner from Next he'd have been made up, but I wanted to spoil him and went overboard on presents. I probably spent a couple of grand on an Apple laptop, Superdry jeans, Louboutin trainers, Tom Ford aftershave, and a load of other bits and pieces. I'd got a stack of family photos from his mum – Paul as a baby, growing up, joining the army, his parents on their wedding day – and had them made into a book. It hadn't cost much, about thirty quid, but he was so touched when he saw it, he was in tears. It was the first time I'd seen him cry and it made me emotional too.

He had gone mad on gifts for me. I got a white Alexander McQueen bag, a pair of navy Jimmy Choo shoes, chocolates from Selfridges, Marc Jacobs' Daisy perfume, a Betty Boop statuette, some lovely ornaments, and a cute teddy bear with 'I love you T' on his front. I thought maybe once we'd opened our presents, Paul would pop the question, but nothing happened. We cleared away the wrapping paper and he started messing about with the laptop while I went into the kitchen to check on dinner. I was thinking, *Any minute now.* I half expected him to come in while I was stirring the gravy and spring a proposal on me. He didn't.

We had lunch, a traditional roast with all the trimmings, and, as we ate, I was all geared up, waiting for him to put down his knife and fork and say he had another present for me, a surprise. Strange, he seemed in no hurry. The day wore on. We had a lie-down in the afternoon. By now, I was getting twitchy. What was stopping him? We got up, had some supper. The day was almost over. I put a face mask on and got into my pyjamas and Paul stretched out on the couch in front of the TV. He didn't look to me like a man on the verge of a marriage proposal. After hours of being patient, I lost it.

'All day I've been waiting for you to say something,' I said.

He looked puzzled. 'What's that, babe?'

'I thought you were going to propose!'

'Propose?' He looked thoroughly confused. 'What with?'

'The ring!'

'*What* ring?'

'The *engagement* ring!'

I had jumped the gun. There was no engagement ring. *Yet*. In fact, he was planning to propose, only not on Christmas Day, and he had already chosen the ring. A few days later we went to get it. It was beautiful, three diamonds on a platinum band. Left to my own devices, I would probably have gone for a single stone, but Paul wanted three to represent 'I love you' and 'past, present, future'. On New Year's Eve, just after midnight, he called me into the bedroom. I sat on the edge of the bed. He seemed a bit distracted, feeling around under the covers, and I wondered what on earth he was doing. Looking for the ring, apparently. Turned out he had hidden it under the duvet and after a few glasses of wine was having trouble finding it.

Eventually, he got down on one knee. 'I love you very much. Will you be my wife?'

Straight away, I was sobbing. Even when you know a proposal's in the offing, it's amazing how moving those few words are. I was overwhelmed. He was my best friend, my lover, my soulmate, my other half in every sense. I loved him so much. It was as if I was seeing the ring properly for the first time. It was perfect. He was right about the three diamonds and when I thought about what they symbolized – *I-love-you. Past-present-future* – I cried even harder. There was nothing I wanted more than to spend my life with him. 'Oh, it's gorgeous, it's lovely,' I said, tears streaming down my face. I spent so long gushing over the ring I forgot about Paul, still on one knee waiting for an answer.

'I'm starting to feel a bit of an idiot down here,' he said. 'Will you just say yes?'

'Yes! YES! Of course I'll marry you!'

I phoned Dannielle in Melbourne. I was nervous breaking the news. It had always been me and her, and I suppose I wanted her approval. She was lovely about it but wary at the same time. In fairness, Dannielle was wary about anyone I got involved with. It wasn't that there was anything she didn't like about Paul, more that she was yet to be convinced the relationship would last.

The next day, 1 January 2010, we started looking at wedding venues. At that stage, we were looking at dates the following year, so there was no urgency. Then my aunty Doreen was diagnosed with ovarian cancer and we decided to bring the wedding forward. I wanted to get married on her birthday, 28 August 2010, which meant we only had a few months to find a venue and get things sorted. What I didn't realize was that this particular Saturday, which fell on the Bank Holiday weekend, was the most requested wedding date in the entire year. Everywhere was booked. When the Hilton Hotel in Manchester had a cancellation and said they could do it, we jumped at it.

With the wedding plans under way, Paul and I went to Jamaica in February 2010. I was enormous, 17 stone 2 pounds, not that much smaller than I had been on that dreadful holiday in Egypt a couple of years earlier. The difference this time was that I was happy. Paul adored me. He knew how important it was for me to lose weight and he was there for me, a hundred per cent, but not once did he put pressure on me or make me feel I wasn't good enough. In his eyes, I was perfect, whatever size I was. We celebrated Valentine's Day with a romantic candlelit dinner on the beach. I was happy and in love, planning my wedding, determined not to be a fat bride. I had rearranged my gastric band procedure for 11 March 2010. Not long before, I did a pre-op photo shoot with *Closer* magazine and looked like a sumo wrestler. Ten days before my op, I was back on the liquids-only diet, then Paul and I headed back to Dolan Park Hospital in the Midlands. At that point I weighed 16 stone 2 pounds and was in size 22 clothes. For some reason, I was even more nervous about the surgery than I had been the previous December. I became paranoid, convinced something would go wrong, and left instructions about my will. I kept texting our Lynn to make sure she knew where to find the briefcase with all my important documents, just in case. A few minutes before I was due to go into theatre, my surgeon, Mr Sigurdsson, came in to see how I was.

'How are you feeling? Ready?'

'I'm absolutely terrified.' That was putting it mildly.

'There's nothing to worry about. You'll be up, walking about, thirty minutes after you come round.'

I wondered whether to say I was worried about not waking up at all, never mind walking around afterwards. 'It's the anaesthetic – it's making me really anxious,' I said.

'Trust me, it's very straightforward. A few hours from now, it's all going to be over.'

I wanted to believe him.

'With your history over the last twenty years, even if you managed to lose all the weight you want to by dieting, I *guarantee* you'd put it all back on. I would bet my house on it.'

He was right. I was sick of being fat, my wedding was less than six months away, and I wanted to look good on my big day. I could diet all I liked and I might well lose a bit of weight, but it would go back on again, like it had all those times before. I'd had enough of the whole yo-yo diet thing. The gastric band was a way of limiting how much I ate and was my best chance, my last chance.

As predicted, soon after coming round I was up and about. The op was a keyhole procedure, so I had four small incisions in my stomach, one slightly bigger than the others where the port was for the band. This was basically an access point for the surgeon, so he could make my band tighter or loosen it off in time, depending on how I was doing. Other than having a dry throat and feeling a bit sore, I was fine. Paul stayed with me overnight and the next day we went home.

For the first four weeks or so I was on liquids while I got used to the band and my stomach healed. Within days I knew it was working, I was losing weight. It was so effective I wondered why I'd waited so long to have it done. A week after the operation I'd lost 9 pounds and felt amazing. After four weeks I was 23 pounds lighter at 14 stone 7 pounds. I had a wardrobe clear-out, gave a load of my fat clothes to the charity shop, and went back to have my band filled. The idea of the fill is to make sure the band is the right size. How it works is by restricting the amount of food you can eat and, because we're all different, it has to be adjusted to meet each individual's needs. I found it was impossible to overeat. After the first few weeks I could eat almost anything, as long as I was sensible about it. I got into the habit of eating little and often, having the same as Paul, except smaller portions – a spoonful of everything, a fraction of what I'd have had before. I never went hungry.

The weight kept falling off. Ten weeks after the operation

I went back to get my band filled a second time. I was down to 13 stone 12 pounds, wearing size 16 clothes, feeling fantastic. I kept going back to have the band adjusted and at one point got a bit carried away and had it so tight I could barely swallow. I stuck with it, thinking I'd be fine. After five days I'd lost 14 pounds, which pleased me no end, but even getting liquids inside me was almost impossible. When I started choking in my sleep, Paul dragged me back to the clinic to get the band loosened.

I settled into my routine of eating well, little and often, having porridge for breakfast, loads of fresh vegetables – spinach, broccoli, cabbage, kale, carrots. I'd have fish most days: sea bass, mackerel, cod, sardines, smoked haddock, or finny haddock, as it's called in Liverpool. I was still eating all the things I loved, like chocolate, Oreos, crisps, just not so much as before. From six packets of crisps at a single sitting, I was down to one packet, two at the most, a week. Instead of half-a-dozen bars of chocolate, I was satisfied with a couple of pieces. It made make think about how much I'd been eating before. I realized I'd got into the habit of serving mountains of food, far too much to be healthy, and it was ridiculous, excessive. At times, Paul pulled me up when I put a meal in front of him. 'Who's that for,' he'd say, 'me and me mates?'

I was busy on *Shameless*, and Paul was working at a children's home where some of the kids came from difficult, disturbed backgrounds. It was challenging, stressful work. Every conversation he had with a child in his care had to be documented. One or two of the lads were teenagers with a history of violence, extreme stuff. Every time he went to work

I was churned up, expecting something bad to happen. He was doing long hours, double shifts, and as I was coming in from *Shameless*, he was on his way out. I hated it. After three or four months of barely seeing each other, I couldn't stand it and asked him to give up the job, which he did and went back to personal training, where the money was a bit more up and down, but at least my mind was at rest and we had more time together.

Within six weeks of getting my gastric band, I started hitting the shops. I'd always loved fashion. I loved spending as well. With me, it was almost a disease. Even when I was enormous I loved shopping. Ten, fifteen years ago, Evans was a great boost for us big birds. The fat shop, I used to call it. I could spend £500 in there on a coat, jeans, a top, a dress. The only thing was, all my dresses were like tents. I'd always loved Marks & Spencer's Per Una range and could happily spend a couple of hundred pounds in there. I couldn't wear any of it, though, I was so big, and I'd end up giving it away. As the weight came off and I was able to wear nice things, I went berserk. I started going into Harvey Nicks and Selfridges and got to know the personal shoppers. In no time, I was a regular, going in once a week, sometimes more. My idea of heaven was to have £3,000 or £4,000 in my bag and go on a spree. I could easily spend a whole day browsing, closeted in a dressing room, trying on clothes. I'd take a friend and give them the complimentary champagne while I had a cappuccino with toffee crisp biscuits. I started to buy a lot of Marc Jacobs and Missoni. I liked Pinko, Armani, Prada, Nicole Fahri, Chanel and Gucci. I got a lot of DKNY dresses and wraps. I spent £1,000 on a Matthew Williamson dress. My big crush was Alexander McQueen. Over the course of a year I probably bought about fifteen pieces. I bought bags by Marc Jacobs, Russell & Bromley, Jimmy Choo, McQueen. My red Fendi was my favourite. I'd seen Kim Cattrall with it in *Sex and the City* and kept going into Selfridges to look at it until finally I splashed out and bought it. I bought shoes by Louboutin, D&G. I fell in love with my Jimmy Choo biker boots. At nearly £600 they weren't cheap, but I could get them soled and heeled every year and the signature emblem re-done, all for free, so I thought they were good value. My mum thought it was far too much to spend on a pair of boots, but my feeling was if you buy cheap, you buy twice.

'We're not all multi-millionaires,' she said.

I wasn't either. I was just living like one.

Anyone would think I had money to burn.

26

I set a budget of £35,000 for the wedding, which seemed like a lot of money until I started making plans and the costs began to spiral. At first, it seemed like a few hundred quid here and there. I'd pick invitations I liked and the price would be £2,000, which seemed a bit steep, so I'd ask how much it would be if I went for the other ones I'd looked at, the less elaborate ones, and it would be £1,800. It hardly seemed worth it for the sake of £200, so I chose the lovely silk ones after all, in cream and red for Liverpool FC, with a John Lennon quote – 'Life's what happens while you're busy making other plans' – on the front, and one of Shakespeare's love sonnets on the back. Of course, I wasn't keeping a tally of how the spending was stacking up. Money seemed unimportant. I wanted my wedding to be wonderful and if I went a bit over budget it wouldn't be the end of the world. I'd taken on a PA, Dawn Goddard, and she turned out to be brilliant. With her on board, I didn't need a wedding planner.

Meanwhile, I was shopping for my wedding dress, still losing weight, feeling good about myself. I was on a mission. I must have tried at least twenty different places, from Vera Wang in London to Dream Brides, a boutique in Walton village, near Liverpool. I wasn't sure exactly what I wanted, although, at forty-seven years old, a meringue was out. Funny, people say when it comes to choosing a wedding dress, you *know* when you've found the right one. After I'd tried on about fifty dresses, all of them lovely, none of them what I wanted, I was thinking, *how* do you know? I ended up in a bridal shop in Cheetham Hill, in Manchester, with Mum and Doreen and our Lynn and Carol for support. It was like one of those TV talent shows, me coming in and out of the dressing room, parading in front of the judging panel, none of the frocks quite hitting the mark. That day, I tried on something like thirty dresses. To say it was exhausting is the understatement of the year. Jan, the woman whose shop it was, was endlessly patient.

Finally, I tried on a dress by a designer called Kate Sherwood. It was Italian silk, champagne coloured, with a sweetheart neckline and a diamante trail across the front. It was simple and understated and lovely. The silk was heavy and rustled when I moved. I put on a floor-length veil scattered with tiny crystals, and a tiara. For a moment or two, I studied my reflection from different angles in the full-length mirrors of the dressing room. Something about this particular dress felt different. I couldn't put my finger on it. Was it the colour – not quite white, not quite ivory? The cut? The way the diamantes caught the light and sparkled? I began to work out what was special about the dress. Wearing it, *I* felt different. When I stepped out of the dressing room, nobody said a word. Then, Doreen and Lynn started crying. *That's* how you know.

I had found the perfect dress for me.

The cost of the wedding kept on going up. Knowing I was only ever going to do it once, I wanted the best of everything. When Paul and I sat down to go through the menus for our formal reception, we chose goat's cheese on rocket and alfalfa with avocado and a light lime dressing to start, followed by fillet of beef with seasonal vegetables and potatoes, and New York cheesecake for afters. Of course, it was the most expensive option. We picked fine wines and Laurent-Perrier rosé champagne, a five-tiered cake that was four-and-a-half feet tall. I booked the Presidential suite at the hotel. My bridesmaids were my nieces, Michaela, Alex and Bobbi, and Paul's cousin Nikki's daughter, Casey. I had two flower girls – my brother Simon's daughter, Leonie, and Paul's cousin, Madison. The little ones were in frothy white frocks, and the bridesmaid dresses were full-length red silk trimmed with cream to match my bridal gown. My nephew Bradley, the only boy in our family, was a page boy, along with Mikey Taylor, the son of our friends Mike and Jo.

We were getting married at one in the afternoon on 28 August 2010, in front of a hundred and fifty guests. In the evening, another five hundred were showing up for the party. I wanted it to be the best wedding anyone had ever been to. We had six bars, three DJs, the biggest buffet the Hilton could do. We booked twelve acts, including Positive

Impact from Toxteth, a youth training and performing arts company, who did everything from Stevie Wonder to Bob Marley and the Jackson 5 and were amazing, and Aidan Davis, the young street dancer who'd got to the final of *Britain's Got Talent* the year before. When I think about the big outgoings, where all the money went, there were a few eye-watering bills. The bill for flowers was nearly £8,000. Matt and Jane, who did those, dressed the room for the reception with 7,500 red roses. Their mantra for the big day was, 'Leave it to us.' What they came up with was out of this world. I spent £11,000 on four chandeliers, a velvet curtain with stars on it and a dance floor, which seemed steep, even to me. I was like, 'Eleven grand – do you get to take them home and keep them, then?' On the night, they looked amazing, worth every penny. The whole thing was perfect, out of this world. Over the top, definitely, but a genuine celebration of love. Thinking about it now, I'd do it all again.

It was always going to be an emotional day. My dad wasn't there to walk me down the aisle and that was a tough one. He'd have loved it. My godmother, my aunty Doreen, who I'd always been close to, had just finished her first bout of chemotherapy. Dannielle was still reticent about the wedding, but that's how she was. If I'd been marrying Brad Pitt, she'd have been the same. I tried to put it all out of my mind and focus on the positives. I started compiling a list of all the things I had to smile about. My uncle Rob was walking me down the aisle. Doreen was there to see me tie the knot – and celebrate her seventy-second birthday. Dannielle was back from her year-long trip. I was having the wedding of my dreams, marrying the man I would spend the rest of my life with. Paul was my everything. I counted my lucky stars we'd found each other.

When I thought back to how I was the year before when we first met, so much had changed. I barely recognized myself. There was a lot less of me, for one thing! Since having the gastric band fitted five months earlier, I had lost 4½ stone and was down to a little over 11 stone. My wedding dress was a size 16. I felt fit and healthy, happier than I'd ever been. As I got ready, had my hair and make-up done and put my dress on, I looked in the mirror. The fatty I had once been was nowhere to be seen. I felt fantastic, ecstatic. As I was about to put my veil on, my mum walked in.

'Imagine if your dad could see you now,' she said.

That's all it took and I dissolved into floods of tears. I would have given anything for him to be there walking me down the aisle. He'd have been so proud. I still missed him so much. I pulled myself together, had my make-up redone, took several deep breaths, and I was ready.

I walked down the aisle along a carpet of thousands of red rose petals, the Beatles song 'Something in the Way She Moves', playing. I was so nervous I could hardly breathe. If I hadn't hung on to my uncle Rob, I think my legs would have gone. Paul looked amazing, so handsome. We exchanged our vows at the very top of the hotel, the highest point in Manchester. In front of us on the glass floor was a heart made from cream roses. As we made our promises I was euphoric, emotional. Below, everything seemed tiny, traffic on Deansgate appearing to move in slow motion. Twenty-three floors down, people went about their business like any other day. We knew different. For us, it was special, the best day. Ever. Our wedding day.

I'd been so busy in the run-up to the wedding, I'd not seen the room for the reception all decked out in red and white and with all the flowers on the tables. It looked amazing, stunning. The food was wonderful, not that I could eat much of it with my gastric band. I managed a tiny bit of beef and it was delicious, but Paul had to finish it for me.

We had loads of speeches, which had everyone laughing and crying. Paul made a speech and so did I. So did Vinny, the best man, and Kerry, my best mate, who cried all the way through hers. Dannielle did a short speech and got tearful when she said she could see how happy Paul made me. My uncle Rob made the shortest speech of all and said if my dad had been there he'd have been so proud and happy. My mum was crying, as were Doreen, Kerry, me and Paul.

After the reception, I told everyone to have a break for a couple of hours. 'My husband will be that drunk tonight and I'll be that tired we won't want to have sex, so we're off to consummate the marriage now,' I said.

Everyone was screaming, 'Get a room!'

We already had!

In the afternoon, Paul had a drink with a couple of his mates and I caught up with my mum and Doreen and Kerry and some of the others. I had a row with Dannielle; I couldn't even tell you what it was about. She'd had a few drinks and was argumentative. All of my friends would say: no change there. It was to be expected, how it always was with us. She had already let me know how she felt by sauntering into the reception late, after the line-up, once everyone else had taken their seats. The problem is Dannielle has never had to share me. Since she was about five, if I'd been going off to a function or a film premiere or whatever and she wasn't coming, she would manage to get ill or fall off her bike or something. It was always about me and her. On my wedding day it was about me and Paul, and it must have been hard for her.

After the wedding, Paul and me had a few days in London. A friend of mine, Mark Fuller, gave us the bridal suite in his hotel in Soho, the Sanctum. It was gorgeous. I took Paul to see *Les Misérables*, my all-time favourite musical, and we had a wonderful time, then I was straight back to work on *Shameless*.

I think in the end the bill for everything came to £96,000. It was the most money I'd ever spent, more than I paid for my house in Widnes. When I think about it like that, it seems excessive, but it was a perfect day. *OK!* magazine and ITV's *Celebrity Four Weddings* covered about half the cost but I had to find the rest. Do I regret it? No. It was the best wedding I'd ever been to – emotional, sentimental, funky, lavish, sexy, cool, trendy, classy – everything I wanted it to be.

What I do regret is not budgeting, and getting myself into debt.

27

My finances were all over the place. The rate I'd been spending, it was no wonder. I wasn't keeping track of how much money was coming in or where it was going. I had no idea what was in my purse from one day to the next, let alone my bank account. If I had money, I spent it. A year after having the gastric band fitted, my weight was down to 9 stone. I was a slim size 10 for the first time in years and loved nothing more than going shopping, spending the day at Harvey Nicks and blowing thousands on clothes or a pair of fabulous shoes. I'd end up bumming a fag off someone when I ran out of cash. I'd never been good at budgeting, but I was getting worse. At home, I had twelve rails packed with lovely designer things, loads more clothes than most people have. My idea of a good time was trying on all my dresses. I didn't need to go anywhere. I was happy staying in, putting on a load of outfits, the kind of clothes I couldn't wear before I lost weight. I loved scarves, waistcoats, jackets, fur coats. Shorts were my favourite. I bought about fifty pairs – suede, silk, smart, casual, fitted, long, short, red, gold, sequined ... shorts with logos, Top Shop beach shorts, Burberry combats, shorts from all over the world. I think the reason I loved them so much was they worked on boys and girls and were sexy and quirky and daft and practical too.

I loved bags as well and probably ended up with about three hundred, some of them with a price tag of £2,000, like my prized red Fendi, or more. My shoe collection was out of this world. I had something like five hundred pairs of boots and shoes and twenty-eight pairs of Uggs in different colours and styles.

I'm ashamed to say that once I started losing weight and getting nice things to wear I spent £150,000 in Harvey Nicks.

The irony was that when I had less money, things were a lot more manageable. It was as if the more success I had, the more money I made, the more I struggled to handle it. As I got busier, my life became ever more complicated. In my line of business, you're not on a salary, and most of the time you don't quite know when you're going to be paid. Some companies were prompt, others kept me waiting months. Aside from *Shameless*, work could be erratic and the amount coming in could vary enormously. Off the top of my head, I have no idea how much I've earned over the years. A lot. It's not always the most prestigious stuff that brings in the most money. One of the most lucrative jobs I ever did was the VW advert in 1991. I was paid in stages and don't remember exactly how much I got, but it was in excess of £50,000. By comparison, that same year I got £800 for appearing in the

Frank Clarke film *Blonde Fist*. Unless you're organized and apply a bit of common sense – which I never had – it was easy to get into trouble. Financially, I was in a mess, keeping things ticking over in a chaotic fashion, hoping everything would work out fine. I had no idea whether my earnings were enough to cover my outgoings. The wedding had put a huge hole in my finances, and Dannielle's year-long trip had also cost a lot more than I expected. She had asked for £7,000–9,000 to cover it, and I agreed, but the expense never stopped. Over a five-year period, what with her trip and rent and everything else, it worked out she cost me £50,000. She swore that wasn't right, but my accountant has all the statements. I'm thinking of getting them stapled together and framed as a reminder.

I was working flat out – long hours on *Shameless*, teaching drama through my company, Be Frank, doing personal appearances here, there and everywhere, theatre work. I needed a small army of people to help me keep on top of things. I had a PA, a gardener, a cleaner, someone to do the laundry, drivers to get me from one job to the next. At one point, I made a list of all the people I was dealing with and there were more than thirty names on it. Thinking about it made my head spin.

It can be hard for the people around me to understand what my life is really like – not that I'm complaining. I know how fortunate I am. Even so, it can look as if my job is all about chauffeur-driven cars, getting my make-up done, red-carpet events, goody bags, prancing about having a lovely time. Some people don't get how busy the work side can be, and when I haven't the time for the normal everyday stuff that other people take for granted, I get vilified and called selfish. I haven't spoken to my brother for two years, after I was late with a birthday card. That was what brought things to a head, anyway. He couldn't understand why I didn't have two minutes to post a card on time, but the truth was I actually didn't. When I was filming *Shameless*, doing twelve-hour days, living in a village where there's no post office, I genuinely struggled with stuff almost everybody else finds simple and straightforward. It would have been easier for me to get in a cab, pay a £60 fare, drive up to my brother and hand over a card in person than to get one in the post. It sounds mad, but it's true. I upset a lot of people over stuff like that; things that didn't seem all that important to me but, at times, drove some of my friends and family mad.

I always had a good time playing Mimi. She was a gift of a character, a dream. Whatever she got up to, I felt safe in the role, knowing I was working with a bunch of talented individuals – cast and crew – and that the show had real integrity. Even when Mimi was at her worst, she was fun, and it was brilliant playing that madness. Where else was I going to get to kidnap people and hold them at gunpoint? Or jump out of cars, trash places, burn down houses? She bottled people, butted them, throttled them, tied them up. I had to laugh when they sent her to anger-management classes. It would take a lot more than that to calm Mimi down.

I was OK with most of what I had to do, although there were some things I struggled with, like the passionate stuff with Michael Taylor, who played my husband, Billy. Michael was young and good-looking and a lot of girls fancied him, but to me he was like a son. It might seem strange, but I actually found doing sex scenes with him a lot easier, less intimate somehow, than ones where we had to kiss. Everybody, including Michael, knew how uncomfortable I found the whole kissing thing. He loved to wind me up. Before one of those scenes I'd threaten him, Mimi-style. 'If you kiss me properly, I'm going to punch you in the cock.' He thought it was hilarious. One scene I'll never forget was when Mimi and Billy came downstairs after having sex and were in the kitchen, Mimi in her nightie sitting on his knee, the two of them snogging, when her sons Jamie (Aaron McCusker) and Micky (Ciaran Griffiths) burst in. We did a rehearsal and it was fine. As soon as we started kissing, the lads got their cue, charged in, and we pulled apart. It was over in a few seconds. I could just about handle it. We went for a take and Michael and I got into a clinch. We started kissing. On set, all was quiet. We kissed some more. No sign of the lads. Something wasn't right. I was starting to feel awkward, sure that any second Simon Turner, the 1st assistant director, would shout, 'Cut!' He didn't. There was definitely something wrong. Finally, I'd had enough and pulled away.

'What's going on?' I said.

The door flew open and Aaron and Ciaran fell in, laughing their heads off. The crew were doubled up; Michael was crying he was laughing so much. They'd all been in on the joke.

'*You fucking bastards!* Do that to me again and I'll punch the lot of you!' I was in full Mimi mode, not that anyone looked remotely scared. They were too busy laughing.

There were always pranks and wind-ups on set. When it came to the dream sequences in *Shameless*, you never knew what you were going to have to do. I had one where Mimi was in bed with Frank and when she turned over and saw him next to her, unwashed and smelly with his awful stringy hair, she screamed the place down. We went for a take. I rolled on to my side and David Threlfall threw back the bed covers to reveal a massive black dildo. I freaked out.

I hated anything that involved walking down stairs. I always had a fear of falling. Show me a staircase and I lose my coordination. I've had a few falls and I suppose they've made me anxious.

Simon Turner used to tear his hair out. 'You don't do stairs, you don't do kissing, you don't do eating any more ...'

With Mimi, almost anything went. She was foul-mouthed, intimidating, vicious. I would sometimes read a script and think she was horrible, that she had no redeeming features at all, but at the same time I understood her. She made sense, to me, anyway, and the audience seemed to love her. I knew as much from the reaction I got when I was out and about. I trusted the writers, the creative team. You often hear actors complaining about the producers and directors they work with, but not on *Shameless*. Ours were brilliant, talented. Everybody involved, from the art department to costume, make-up, cameras, lighting, sound – they all knew what they were doing. Jo Slater, head of wardrobe, became a very good friend, as did Rachael Bryant, who did my make-up. I felt challenged, pushed to the limit. The standard was always high. Over the years, *Shameless* won BAFTAs, Emmys, RTS awards, British Comedy Awards. It swept the board here and in other countries.

At *Brookside*, I had felt underused. *Shameless* was a different story. Paul Abbott and George Faber gave me more and more to do until, in the end, I was in more than a hundred episodes. I got to work with some wonderful actors in the show – Angeline Ball (Gloria), Karen Bryson (Avril), Bex Atkinson (Karen), Sally Carman (Kelly), Isy Suttie (Esther), Sue Vincent (Derilee), Clare Higgins (Hazel), Clive Mantle (Mr Banbury), James Dreyfus (the school inspector), Stephen Lord (Dominic), Dean Lennox Kelly (Kev), Bob Pugh (Malcolm); the list goes on – and learned so much from Becky Ryan, the young girl who played Debbie Gallagher. She was dealing with graphic adult humour and handled it so well, with such maturity, I was gobsmacked. She was gifted and unaffected and incredibly well behaved on set, and it made me think she must have had really good parenting. I also made some great friendships, especially with Isy and Angeline and Sue.

I had no idea I was going to spend almost ten years playing Mimi. Getting the part turned things round and gave me stability, regular work, a good income – even if I was hopeless at managing it.

Money was burning a hole in my pocket. All my working life, I'd had my ups and downs with it, splashing out on things I couldn't afford, racking up debts, getting into trouble, having run-ins with credit card companies, bailiffs knocking on the door.

In 2012, things came to a head.

28

I still owed more than £30,000 to the friend who'd stumped up the cash a few years earlier to help me finish my film, *Reuben, Don't Take Your Love To Town.* When she got in touch and asked for the money back, I didn't have it. At one time, we'd been close. She had saved my arse and I'd saved hers, more than once. Now our friendship was broken beyond repair. It was my fault. I had been irresponsible, and she decided to take me to court. Fair enough, although it meant I would be made bankrupt. No amount of juggling my finances or hoping for the best this time was going to make the slightest difference.

I don't mean to sound flippant, because bankruptcy is a big deal, but, for me, it wasn't the end of the world. I had a job, money coming in, and was fully intending to pay back what I owed. I even thought that maybe it was the kick up the backside I needed where money was concerned. Still, I dreaded telling Paul. In his world you earned a salary, got paid a certain amount on a set date, and lived within your means, which was about as far removed from how I lived my life as possible. I picked my moment, after he'd had a few glasses of wine, and kept the conversation brief, told him I was being taken to court over an unpaid debt, that they would add in everything else I owed and I'd be made bankrupt. I stressed it was nothing to worry about because I'd pay it all back. I glossed over things, really, not wanting him to worry, especially when there was nothing he could do about it.

Before any of this blew up, Paul and I had booked to go to Los Angeles, where I had business meetings set up. It was his thirtieth birthday and I wanted to make it special, so I tagged on a week in Hawaii as a surprise because I knew it was the one place in the world he had always wanted to see. It was already arranged and paid for before there was any inkling of me being made bankrupt.

It was my first trip to LA and I couldn't wait. It's the city at the heart of the movie industry, where all the studios are, and it has a reputation, a buzz. After I'd been there a couple of days, I hated it. It wasn't the star-studded creative hub I expected at all. There was something shabby, slightly seedy about it. We stayed in the Roosevelt Hotel, a historic place on Hollywood Boulevard, right in the heart of things. You stepped out of the door and onto the Walk of Fame. Close by was the Dolby Theatre, where the Oscars are held, and the famous Chinese Theatre with the hand- and footprints of the stars set into the pavement, or sidewalk, as the Americans call it. That was something I really wanted to see, but I couldn't have been more disappointed. The handprints were dirty, there were cracks in the pavement, and the area seemed to be a magnet for homeless people. It all felt a bit sad and sorry and down at heel. We wandered along the Walk of Fame and stood beside Johnny Depp's star. A few yards away a man lay sprawled on the ground, out of it. Everywhere you looked there were people on their uppers. I had never seen anything like it.

The hotel was like something out of a Jackie Collins novel, Porsches lined up outside, beautiful young things – and a few big ugly horrors – drinking Cristal champagne, hanging out by the pool with its underwater mural by David Hockney. The Roosevelt had lots of connections to the movie industry. Marilyn Monroe lived there for a couple of years, and a penthouse suite was named after Clark Gable and Carole Lombard, who had stayed there. The hotel was a location for some of the scenes from the Leonardo diCaprio film *Catch Me If You Can* and the TV series *Entourage*, and the first Academy Awards ceremony in 1929 was held there. The Roosevelt had a reputation as a cool, party hotel and there always seemed to be champagne flowing. At the same time, you'd have thought there was a world shortage of cigarettes, because I was the only person who ever had any. I'd be minding my own business, lounging by the pool with my book, and some total stranger would come up and ask to bum a fag.

'Excuse me, ma'am, could I get one of those cigarettes?'

It got on my nerves. Eventually, I snapped. 'If you can afford to drink Cristal, buy your own cigarettes!'

I swear to God that everybody I spoke to in LA was in the movie business, from the people hanging round the hotel pool to the waiters, bar staff, cab drivers ... *everybody*. They were either actors (out of work), writers (busy on a screen-play) or 'in development', which could have meant anything. They all seemed like complete phonies to me. One day, I let off steam to the guy at the hotel reception, who seemed nice enough.

'If one more person tells me they're "resting" or "in development", I'm going to scream,' I said.

He did one of those nervous laughs. 'Actually, *I'm* an actor. I moved here from Wisconsin and right now I'm between jobs so I thought I'd fill in here until something else comes up and ...'

I was gone before he finished the sentence.

Paul Abbott was sure they'd love me in LA. I wasn't convinced. I thought they might find me a bit of an oddball. The meetings I had didn't fill me with confidence. I didn't feel as if I fitted in or as if I wanted to. I tried to imagine spending months there looking for work and I couldn't. The thought of it made me thoroughly depressed. It got to the point where someone asked me what I thought of LA.

'How do you like our city?' he said. 'Don't you think it's full of movers and shakers?'

'More like wankers and wannabes,' I said.

Me and my big mouth.

We put LA behind us and flew to Oahu to spend a week on Waikiki Beach, in Honolulu, which was mind-blowing. Hawaii was without doubt the best place we'd ever been to. It had the tack and playground feel of Vegas, and then, fifteen minutes out of town, it was lush and green and unspoiled. The people were friendly and it felt safe, even walking back to the hotel in the early hours after we'd been out. It was exactly what we needed. The sea was a brilliant shade of turquoise, crystal clear.

For me, the highlight of the trip was the day we went diving with sharks. It was something I had always wanted to do. I find sharks fascinating – graceful, powerful, and with an amazing aura. I know opinion is divided and some people find them horrible and ugly and frightening. I don't suppose the film *Jaws* did much for their image. Personally, I couldn't wait to see them close up. The boat took us three miles off-shore and we got into a cage that was lowered into the sea and pushed out so that the sharks could swim between us and the boat. It was so choppy that day the whole trip was touch and go, and none of the other women on board wanted to get in when the time came. Once we were in the water, we were tossed about inside what felt like quite a flimsy structure with no top on it. Waves broke above our heads and it struck me that there was nothing to stop the sharks getting in with us if they felt like it. I could feel the adrenalin pumping through my body. At one point I counted twenty-one sharks around us, a mix of Galapagos and sandbar, some only inches away. It was phenomenal, emotional, one of the best things I've ever done.

We flew back from Hawaii to Marbella for a photo shoot, which was a work trip and didn't cost me a penny. While we were there I got a call from Dawn, my PA, to say I'd been declared bankrupt. It was May 2012. At the same time, the *Sun* had sent a photographer to snatch pictures of me and Paul supposedly living it up in Spain, not a care in the world. We were all over the papers. The pictures made it look as if I was sticking two fingers up to the bankruptcy hearing, which wasn't the case, since I hadn't known the hearing was going to be held while we were away.

After we'd been there a couple of days, I went to get money from a cash machine, only to have my bank card refused. I assumed it was to do with the bankruptcy but actually it wasn't. Basically, I hadn't told my bank I'd be in Marbella and their anti-fraud system kicked in and cancelled the card. I had no cash. In desperation, I sent a text message to eight close friends asking for help. The text said something like: 'If I've texted you you're one of my best people. I'm desperate for money until I get back to England. Can anyone get me £200? I'm skint, stuck in Marbella, and my card's been swallowed. Please ring the hotel on this number ...'

The next day the text message appeared in the *Sun*. A 'close friend' was quoted as saying they were tired of the situation and that I needed to manage my money better. Hopefully, with the bankruptcy, I'd stop spending, blah, blah. I was absolutely devastated. I couldn't get it out of my head that someone I trusted, one of my closest friends, would sell me out to a newspaper. I was shocked and angry. I had no idea who would do such a thing.

Paul and I were due to spend a few more days away, but then I got a call from *Shameless* to say I had to come back for the BAFTAs at the Royal Festival Hall in London on 27 May. They arranged flights and put us up in the Grosvenor House Hotel. I was told I didn't need to do the press call because of all the hoo-ha over being made bankrupt, but I thought it was better to face the media than hide away. Might as well get it over with. On the red carpet, which was actually a Union Jack, I had on a £1,000 Matthew Williamson dress, a pair of Fendi shoes, a Louboutin clutch, and an Alexander McQueen necklace that was worth a fortune. I'd bought the dress ages before when I was too fat to get into it in the hope that one day I'd be thin enough to wear it. Finally, I was. Paul was in a Hugo Boss suit. We were tanned and glowing from being away and I was a slim size 10, so I felt great about that. I knew how it would look, the pair of us posing and smiling, as if we were taking the piss. To be honest, if I'd had my way I'd have stayed in Marbella, well away from the BAFTAs, but my bosses at *Shameless* were adamant I had to be there. I steeled myself for someone to ask about me being broke, but it was all over-the-top friendly.

'How are you, Tina?'

'You look great!'

'You've lost loads of weight!'

'What have you been up to?'

I told them I'd been in LA, done a few meetings, kept a big smile on my face, sure somebody was about to stick the boot in and ask how it felt to be skint. Nobody said a word about it. As they snapped away and got their pictures, I kept smiling. If no one else was going to mention it, I thought I should.

'As you know, things have been a bit up and down, *what with me being made bankrupt last week*, so I thought I'd put on a show, get dressed up, make myself feel a bit better.' They all howled.

For the next couple of weeks I fretted about the text message that had ended up in the *Sun* and got totally paranoid. This is where my bipolar disorder comes into play, where something I can't make sense of gets hold of me and my mania kicks in. I could *not* stop thinking about it. It went round and round inside my head, gnawing away at me. It caused rows with Paul, who's extremely laid-back, the kind of person who can get upset and go off the rails about something for two minutes or so and then forget all about it. Not me. I dwell and dwell and just about drive myself insane. It got so I'd wait for him to go to bed and then sit up half the night making lists, trying to work out who had done the dirty on me. I'd focus on one person at a time and for twenty-four hours solid would hound them. When I didn't get anywhere I'd move on to the next name on the list. Paul told me to let it go, but I couldn't.

'Are you sure you only sent it to those eight people?' he said.

I was sure.

I never did get to the bottom of the text message that ended up in the paper, or at least nobody actually owned up. I have a pretty good idea who it was, not that I think it was done out of malice. I'm guessing what happened was a reporter got in touch for a comment about the bankruptcy and, not thinking, my so-called friend blabbed without meaning to. It happens. It took me a while but I finally let that one go.

For Paul's thirtieth I got him a puppy, a cocker spaniel. I wanted that particular breed because when he was a soldier in Iraq, those were the dogs trained to detect improvised explosive devices. The puppy was gorgeous, the cutest little thing. I wanted to call her Barbra because she had a look of Streisand about her. Paul put his foot down.

'I'm not standing on the Green shouting for Barbra,' he said.

We called her Bella instead. She was adorable but, God in heaven, she was naughty. She chewed the TV remote, shoes, the leather couch . . . anything she could get her teeth into. Bob, my little Yorkie, who's posh and proper and well behaved, looked on, bemused. I told myself that once she was out of the puppy phase she'd calm down. More than a year on, she's big, strong and boisterous – and a real Daddy's girl. While Bob loves nothing more than snuggling up beside me on the sofa listening to the Carpenters, Bella's idea of a good time is rolling round the floor with Paul, mock fighting, to a soundtrack of Tupac and Biggie.

Oh, and she still chews the furniture.

29

I had been playing Mimi for the best part of ten years. I loved her, *Shameless* had been good to me, and I was proud to be part of such a brilliant, award-winning show. Mimi had seen me through some tough times. She was there during my darkest moments. When I was at my fattest and most depressed, I took refuge in her. A lot of the time, I was more her than me and, when I couldn't see the point of living, she kept me going. Even when I'd been to hell and back, I'd turn up for work and give a hundred per cent. Sometimes, I don't know where I'd have been without the discipline of a schedule, having lines to learn, not wanting to let people down. For me, the made-up world of the Chatsworth Estate with all its craziness was a lifesaver. On set, I was safe, surrounded by good, kind, talented people. Even at my lowest ebb, I could go to work and for the next few hours at least put what was going on in the outside world to the back of my mind. She was so much a part of my life, it was hard to imagine being without her. At times I thought I was turning into her. Walking along the street in Manchester one day with Paul, one of the lads in front of us dropped a fast-food carton on the ground and I roared.

'That's *disgusting*! There's a fucking bin there! What's wrong with you? Your own city!'

They turned round and looked completely shocked. 'It's Mimi! You're a legend.'

'Well, pick up your fucking carton them and get it in the bin, you fucking tramp!'

He did, too.

I walked on with Paul as if nothing had happened.

As much as I loved my job and playing Mimi, I also wanted a baby. I was nearly forty-nine and Paul and I had been married a couple of years.

It was something we had talked about when we first got together. A few months after the wedding, we'd gone privately to the Liverpool Women's Hospital to see Charles Kingsland, one of the top fertility experts in the country. He had a phenomenal reputation for helping women struggling to conceive for all kinds of reasons – age included. I was already way past the cut-off age for IVF treatment on the NHS, which was thirty-five then, although now it's forty-three. I underwent tests to see whether I still had eggs and what kind of condition they were in. It turned out I did but was advised against using them because they weren't in a great state and there was a risk that any child I had might not be healthy. In Mr Kingsland's view, my best bet, my only safe option, really, was egg donation.

Up until then, I'd not even considered it as a possibility and wasn't sure how I felt about it. My first thought was: if it wasn't my egg, was it somehow less my baby? Did it matter that any child we had would have Paul's DNA but not mine? There was a lot to take in and think about. Paul and I went away and talked it over. I told him I was reluctant about using an egg donor and he understood why. It's one of those things where there's no right or wrong answer; it's about doing whatever feels right for you. Different people view the whole idea of egg donation in different ways. Some I spoke to said they felt it made no difference, others did. Initially, Dannielle had her doubts. 'Doesn't it mean it's not your baby?' she said. Did it? Paul was fantastic and gave me space to do all the thinking I needed to. I took my time and never felt under any pressure. We both knew that if we went ahead with IVF, we had to be on the same wavelength.

Of course, there was no guarantee I'd actually get pregnant. I knew women who'd been through IVF, some of them half-a-dozen times or more, and ended up disappointed. It's never something any woman embarks on lightly. When you decide to go down that road it's because you know it's your only hope, so there's already an element of pressure. There's always a chance it won't work and you won't get your happy ending. However prepared you think you might be, the sense of disappointment when it doesn't work out and there's no baby at the end of the process can be devastating. I know, because I've spoken to women who've been there and say the psychological impact of it not going to plan is by far the most difficult thing to cope with.

Paul and I first went to the private UK CFA clinic in

Liverpool to see a colleague of Charles Kingsland, Mr Rafet
Gazvani, in 2011. His opinion was also that egg donation was
right for us. I told him I had reservations, which he understood, but went on to say that all the evidence shows that life
is 70 per cent nurture and 30 per cent nature. Even though
the baby wouldn't have my DNA, it would have my blood
flowing through it, giving it life, as it grew inside me.

'All the nutrients, everything the baby needs to develop, will
come from you, its mother,' he said. 'People talk about blood
being thicker than water. Well, it's *your* blood running through
your child's veins.'

I liked the idea of that. He also explained that the genetic
profile inherited from the parents is by no means a simple
fifty-fifty split and that often there's substantially more of one
parent in a baby's make-up than another. I'd never thought
about that before.

'So I could have ninety per cent of my dad's genes and
only ten per cent of my mum's?' I said.

It was entirely possible, which is where nurture comes in.
Just because you have fewer genes from one parent doesn't
mean you don't take after them. When I was growing up, I
didn't look like either of my parents, yet my brother, Simon,
with his blond hair and blue eyes, was the image of both of
them, if that makes sense. You could see straight away where
he got his looks. Even though I didn't have my dad's looks, as
far as character went, there was no doubt I was his daughter.
I sounded like him and had all his mannerisms. Even now,
people say they can hear Frank in the way I speak. As I've got
older, I've started to look much more like my mother and can
even hear her in the way I speak sometimes, too.

'Nurture is so important,' Mr Gazvani said. 'I guarantee that even using donor eggs, any child you have will take after you because you're such a strong personality. People will be in no doubt it's your child.'

With older women, the clinic's usual cut-off date for IVF was fifty and, at that point, I was coming up to forty-nine so I didn't have time on my side. If we wanted to go ahead, we'd have to get moving. We came away feeling reassured, more positive about the whole process. I was starting to get my head around the idea of egg donation.

When I first met Paul, I was open about everything. I didn't want us having any secrets. Your husband should know every freckle on your arse, all the ins and outs of what makes you tick mentally, emotionally, physically. It was a case of no-holds-barred for me and Paul. I think that's what makes a relationship work. I know not everybody feels the same. I've met women who say there are things they can't talk to their husbands about, important stuff like wanting a baby, and I really don't get it. Isn't your husband the one person you can say anything to?

When I was in my twenties I had two abortions, and I wanted Paul to know about them. The first one was when Dannielle was about eight months old. Once I realized I was pregnant, I knew I wasn't going to have the baby. I didn't have to think long and hard about it or talk it through with the guy I was seeing. We weren't serious anyway and it was my decision. I was eight weeks gone when I had the termination at a clinic in Birmingham. All I remember about it was being on a ward with a few other girls, going off one by one to have the procedure, and nobody talking. I stayed in overnight and came home the next day. It wasn't traumatic and I didn't feel guilty in the way some women do.

I got pregnant again when I was twenty-three. Again, there was no soul-searching about what to do. I didn't want hordes of illegitimate kids. I had my daughter, who meant everything to me. She was five and in private school and I didn't want anything to jeopardize her future. I borrowed £160 from my dad and booked into a clinic in Liverpool for another termination. Again, I didn't talk it over with the guy I was seeing, didn't even mention that I was pregnant. I didn't see the point. It wasn't as if the relationship was going anywhere. Wrong man, wrong time.

When I was pregnant with Dannielle I was a kid of eighteen and, stupidly, thought I was in love with Jimmy and that we could have a life together. I know there's a whole debate around abortion, but I did what was right for me and for my daughter at the time. I do think it's the woman's decision, unless you're in a long-term, stable relationship. Looking back, I don't regret what I did, nor do I feel any sadness or shame. I've had friends who have had abortions and never really got over them. Ten years later, they still feel desolate, and grieve for the child they chose not to have. I totally respect their feelings, but it wasn't like that for me. When I was twenty-six and studying at Childwall College, I had a miscarriage. I hadn't even realized I was pregnant. It probably sounds as if I was careless and irresponsible, but actually I wasn't. Accidents happen. I wanted Paul to know all about it, no surprises, and he was fine. He has never judged me.

Series eight of *Shameless* in 2011 ran for twenty-two episodes, eight more than the previous year. It was fantastic and the show was buzzing. Another twenty-one episodes were scheduled for 2012. I was flat-out busy, cramming as much as I could into every waking moment, as usual.

There wasn't time to think about much beyond work.

30

I wanted a baby. I wanted to try for one, at least, to give me and Paul the best possible chance of having a child of our own. For a couple of months I turned things over inside my head, weighed up the pros and cons, thought about what was really important to me. In the summer of 2012, I got a call from Jemma, at the UK CFA clinic. It was a while since Paul and I had seen Mr Gazvani and she knew that my fiftieth birthday – the cut-off date for treatment – was only a few months away. It was the nudge we needed to start thinking seriously about IVF again. I had come round to the idea of egg donation, so that was no longer a stumbling block. If I did have a baby, I wanted to give it the best chance of being healthy. *If.* That still left one big decision – what to do about work. It would be impossible to have a baby and continue with *Shameless*.

Something was going to have to give.

I did a lot of talking to my dad. I always had, since his death, and found it a comfort. It helped me get things straight in my mind, feeling that he was around, watching over me.

10 August 2012, would have been my dad's eightieth birthday. For the first few years after he died I wouldn't work that day or on the anniversary of his death, then I decided I needed to move on. That day, I'd been busy on *Shameless* and it was late when I got in, gone ten o'clock. As soon as I opened the door, I heard a Frank Sinatra song playing. I went through to the conservatory where Paul was waiting. He had written FRANK in tea lights and put a cigar, a glass of whisky and a handkerchief on the side for my dad. It was perfect, a wonderful way to take a moment and think about him. We had two Chinese lanterns and when it got to midnight we went into the front garden, lit them and let them go. The first one soared into the sky and took off. The second one stayed low, drifted across the road and got stuck in a tree opposite. Paul and I looked at each other. It kept burning. We waited for the tree to catch fire.

'Oh my God, I think we're going to have to call the fire brigade,' I said.

Paul said to give it a minute, see what happened. Gradually, the flames died down and went out. I breathed a sigh of relief.

'That's me dad!' I said.

I felt my priorities begin to shift. You can't be half-hearted about wanting a baby, not at my age. I came to a decision. I was going to have to leave *Shameless*. It took weeks before I plucked up the courage to speak to Jean Holdsworth, the executive producer. Every time I thought about telling her, I lost my nerve. Eventually, in between scenes one day, I called her into my dressing room and said I wanted to leave. I didn't tell her about wanting a baby, just that I thought it was time to hang up my hair extensions and get rid of the acrylic nails. I was due straight back on set and the last thing I wanted was to get tearful, but I couldn't help it. *Shameless* was such a massive part of my life. I was attached to the show and the people working on it. I explained I'd been thinking things over for a while and that my mind was made up. Jean was great, made it easy, said she understood and respected my decision. For the time being, she asked me to keep it quiet and I did. The only other people I told were one of the writers, Jimmy Dowdall, who was in the building that day and bumped into me when I was feeling a bit emotional, and David Threlfall, who had always been so good to me. I knew I could trust him to keep it to himself. He said he didn't blame me for wanting to go.

A few weeks later, in October, 2012, in the middle of shooting scenes, we were told to stop and the entire cast and crew were summoned to the studio floor. It was strange. Nothing like that had ever happened before. My first thought was that it had to be something serious to halt production. Jean Holdsworth was waiting to speak to us.

'We're pulling the plug,' she said. 'This will be the last series we do, so we're going to do a few specials and a big finale. There's a press release going out in a few minutes but I wanted to let you know first.'

She was in tears and so were a lot of the cast and crew. Nobody had seen it coming. A lot of the people who worked on *Shameless* had been with the series from the start. It was going to leave a huge hole in their lives. I was shocked but at the same time glad that Paul Abbott, the creator, had decided the time had come to throw in the towel. It felt right that *Shameless*, a massively successful series with a phenomenal reputation, bowed out with dignity. If we'd been dumped by the channel, I'd have hated it. So, I was leaving, but so was everybody else. A tiny part of me felt relieved to think it wasn't going on without me, after all.

I woke up one morning to find angry red welts running up my legs, my arms, my stomach, across my back. My whole body was covered. It made me think of Michael Gambon in the BBC drama *The Singing Detective*. I went into make-up at *Shameless* and said I'd been scratching all night. I lifted up my top. 'What do you think that is?' I said.

Rachael Bryant, my make-up artist, was horrified. 'Oh my God, I've got no idea,' she said. 'You need to get it looked at.'

Simon Turner, the 1st AD, called a doctor, who came on set and examined me. He suspected it was some kind of allergic reaction. It seemed to subside and I hoped that was the end of it. In fact, it was just the beginning. I started to get regular flare-ups that came out of nowhere. I could be at home watching TV and I'd start to feel my skin get prickly, as if something was crawling up my arms and legs. Within half an hour my entire body would be covered in itchy lumps and bumps. It affected me in different ways at different times. I could have a bad attack and within twenty-four hours it would be gone. For a week or so I'd be fine and think I'd seen the back of it, then it would start up again, usually at night.

Sometimes I'd be asleep and Paul would have to wake me because I was scratching. I went through a phase of having severe attacks for several nights on the trot. I'd be sitting in a lukewarm bath at three in the morning, knowing I had to be up at five to go into work, hysterical, trying not to claw at my skin. I scratched myself so badly I tore the skin all around my neck. The rash was everywhere – even on my fingers and toes. The only place I never got it was on my face. According to the girls in make-up at *Shameless*, that was the actress in me . . .

I knew it wasn't an allergy. I hadn't changed my soap powder, I wasn't using new products on my skin, I hadn't eaten anything out of the ordinary. Eventually, I went to see a specialist in Cheshire. On the way there in the car I had a flare-up, and by the time I stepped into his clinic I was having a full-blown attack.

'It's urticaria,' he said, and put me on a course of strong steroids and antihistamines.

I'd never heard of urticaria. Apparently, it's also known as hives, and happens when high levels of histamine and other chemicals in the body get released into the skin. In my case, it was probably stress-related, which made sense. I'd been made bankrupt, I'd decided to leave *Shameless*, and I wanted to try for a baby. I suppose there was quite a lot going on.

31

I've always pushed myself, even when I was working all the hours on *Shameless*. At times, I went to crazy lengths to fit in a couple of days' filming on something else, or a play. In 2011, I was doing *Rita, Sue and Bob Too* at the Theatre Royal, in St Helens. I would come off set at seven; Janine, my driver, would have the car ready to whisk me straight to the theatre, and, at seven-thirty, I'd be on stage playing downtrodden Michelle with a Yorkshire accent. It was tight and every night I made it by the skin of my teeth. David Threlfall used to see me racing out of the building and go, 'You're insane,' as I disappeared out the door.

It was worth it, though. Paul had been doing a bit of TV-extra work in between the personal training and was coming along to my drama classes, watching me teach, joining in here and there, and *Rita, Sue and Bob Too* was his first play. He was cast after coming to the read-through with me and reading in to help out the director, Sylvie Gatrill, who was so impressed she gave him the part. Dannielle was also in it, so it meant a lot to me. Also, a very good friend of mine, Franny Bennett, who was in the film *Shooters*, had been cast as Bob although, sadly, he had to pull out for personal reasons. It was one of the few plays I'd done where I wasn't first on stage. I'd stand in the wings watching my husband as Sam in mad eighties clothes and a wig flirting with another woman, and then my daughter in the role of Rita, having sex in a car. It was surreal.

How the stress of trying to juggle my many commitments never put Simon Turner, the 1st AD on *Shameless*, in hospital, I'll never know. He was a good lad, really special, and saved my skin – loads of times. I used to plead with him to reschedule when I had to be in London for some filming or other and he'd be tearing his hair out. I'm sure people used to wonder what on earth was going on when he sent round a revised schedule that made no sense to anyone but me.

For years, I was dead against reality TV, then it got to the point there was so much of it about I thought if you can't beat them, join them. I had a good time on *Celebrity Big Brother* and *Celebrity Four Weddings*, so I agreed to do *Celebrity Come Dine With Me*. I love cooking and it's a funny show so I thought it would be a laugh. It actually proved a real eye-opener. When the producers asked me to describe the kind of people I wouldn't want to sit round a dinner table with, I was my usual outspoken self. 'I can't stand ex-soap stars, ones that haven't worked for ten years and done car crash TV, glamour girls who have affairs with footballers, singers who had a couple of hits in the eighties and weren't hip then and certainly aren't now ...'

They put me with Paul Danan, who'd gone from *Hollyoaks* to *Celebrity Love Island*, Imogen Thomas, whose affair with Ryan Giggs had catapulted her into the headlines, and David Van Day from the eighties pop group Dollar. My worst nightmare, in one room, in other words. Talk about a learning curve. Imogen Thomas turned out to be a beautiful, intelligent girl and we became good friends. Paul Danan had been through the mill with drink and drugs and was such a lovely guy I wanted to adopt him. David Van Day was the biggest surprise. On the face of it, he represented everything I hated about eighties music, but turned out to be good company. Cheesy and camp, yes, but genuine and big-hearted too. I'm always suspicious of people who don't like dogs, so when I saw David at home with his Yorkies I was totally won over.

The programme was being recorded in October, 2011, and I was busy on *Shameless*. I'd assumed I'd be hosting my dinner party at home in Manchester, but because everybody else was based in London they wanted me to do it down there. I couldn't. I'd already had to beg favours off Simon Turner to fit in the filming dates in the first place. 'You'll be the death of me,' he said, and I was worried I really would. I couldn't put him through any more stress. I said they would have to come to me, which threw their schedule out, but it couldn't be helped.

For my starter, I made a traditional Liverpool dish, Scouse lamb broth, with potatoes and barley and vegetables, something my mum and nan always made. I served a classy little salad with lobster tails, scallops and smoked haddock on the side. David Van Day thought that was a bit of a cheat. My main course was a three-meat roast with gammon in cherry cola, chateaubriand rolled in parmesan and rosemary and thyme, and chicken in garlic, stuffed with mozzarella – all served with roast potatoes, peppers, sugared carrots and honeyed parsnips. For dessert, I made a New York cheesecake, which tasted good but didn't look all that great. I won the show, had a brilliant time doing it, and made some good friends.

I'd always thought I was quite liberal in my views, but doing *Come Dine With Me* made me realize I could be judgemental. I'm a lot less likely to jump to conclusions now than I might once have been, although I think we all do it to some extent. It happens to me all the time. I know I have a reputation for being ruthless, and a couple of actors have said they were terrified of working with me. I don't know why, as I'm always being told how easygoing and amiable I am. Maybe if you're loud and opinionated it's assumed you're also a nightmare. Or perhaps they're expecting Mimi.

Coming up to Christmas 2012, I took on far too much. I was used to pushing myself, working ridiculous hours, but I got into a proper mess. On top of *Shameless*, I decided to do panto and the new ITV reality series, *Splash!* Everything was happening at the same time, so it was always going to be tight, but I had debts and bills to pay and the bottom line was we needed the money. The year before, I'd played the Wicked Queen in *Snow White* at the Royal Court in Liverpool and loved it, working with Jane Joseph, a director who's famous for her pantos and always gets big names, including Hollywood stars like Mr T. I asked if I could do another one and got the part of the Fairy Godmother in *Cinderella*, at the Theatre Royal in St Helen's. Jane's daughter, Chantelle

Nolan, was directing, and I was looking forward to doing a panto where I wasn't the baddie for a change. By then I was a very slim size 10 and my costume was a lovely little ball-gown.

I was getting ready for panto, working long hours on *Shameless* – and dashing off to Plymouth and Luton to spend time with Tom Daley getting ready for *Splash!* When I think about it now it was sheer madness, but at the time I truly thought I could handle the pressure. I don't think anyone realized how huge *Splash!* was going to be. I certainly didn't. I hadn't taken into account how scary it would be, either. I'm nervous of heights to start with, so you can imagine how I felt about diving into a pool. It was terrifying.

The first time I met Tom Daley he took me up to the ten-metre diving platform. Just getting up there was an ordeal. I felt sick and dizzy by the time I reached the top. Tom was with me every step of the way, calm and confident, full of encouragement. Then again, he'd spent half his life on the ten-metre platform, so it was practically a second home for him.

'Do you want to walk to the edge, just get a feel for it?' he said.

My legs were like jelly. 'Are you having a laugh?'

'It's OK, I used to get scared as well,' he said. 'You'll be fine, really. I'll coach you.'

'Listen, Tom, I've got bras older than you. You're not going to talk me into standing on the edge.'

It didn't exactly make me feel better when he explained that if you hit the water at the wrong angle it's like smashing into a block of concrete.

My mother thought I was mad signing up for a show that meant appearing on Saturday night primetime television in a bathing suit. That was the least of my worries. What really bothered me was managing the overwhelming number of commitments I had. I was supposed to train for a couple of weeks for *Splash!*, but no amount of shuffling things about freed up the time, so I made do with five days. The training was torture. They'd make us all line up at the edge of the pool and one of the trainers would walk along the line and tap someone and they'd have to jump in. No hesitation. I was working with some great people – Linda Barker, Caprice, Donna Air – none of whom seemed to have a problem. Me, I was a bag of nerves. What was I thinking, saying I'd do something that frightened the life out of me?

I started to fret about not being able to manage everything I'd signed up for. We'd get the schedule for *Shameless* and I'd think I could just about work around it and still manage the panto, still make the training sessions for *Splash!*, then we'd get changes through on *Shameless* and, barring a miracle, I couldn't see how I could fit everything in. The stress got so bad my urticaria kicked off. Every bit of me was covered in sore, itchy hives and I felt really poorly. I was scratching all the time, constantly aware of it, not able to sleep. I tried my trick of sitting in a warm bath in the middle of the night, hoping it would soothe my skin, but as soon as I got out the itching was as bad as ever. I wanted to claw at myself to try and get some relief. It was one thing playing Mimi, because at least I was covered up, but the state my skin was in I couldn't imagine going on stage every night as the Fairy Godmother in a little dress. The thought of wearing a swimsuit on TV when my whole body was covered in hives was also distressing me.

The more I stressed, the worse my skin got. It was my own fault for trying to do too much. I tied myself in knots trying to work out how to manage *Shameless* and *Cinderella* and *Splash!*, and sat at home sobbing, crying my eyes out.

'I can't cope, I can't do it.'

Paul was fantastic. 'If you can't cope, it's OK, you don't have to do it,' he said.

My work ethic drove me on until I almost went into meltdown. In the end, I did something I had never done before and said I'd have to miss the first few days of panto.

I just wasn't well enough.

Once I started in panto, Leanne Campbell, a DJ from Liverpool's Juice FM, who was playing Cinderella, asked me to do an interview for her radio show. I couldn't see why not. We chatted for few minutes in the dressing room about what seemed like innocuous enough stuff, not the slightest bit controversial. It all felt very relaxed and informal and she recorded it on her mobile phone. No big deal. Or so I thought. I talked about *Shameless* ending, how cleverly written and directed it was, and said that even though it dealt with explicit themes it was consistently excellent, pure class, that the fan mail we got proved the show appealed to people from all backgrounds. So far, so good. When it came to *Splash!*, what I had to say was less complimentary. I called it garbage, celebrity dross, and said I did it for the coin.

The next day, it was all over the papers. You can imagine how that went down. *Splash!* was a hit show, getting huge ratings and I was rubbishing it. Talk about biting the hand that feeds. Boy, did I regret that interview. I hadn't meant it to come across the way it did, but I should have known better. You'd think after all my years in the business I'd have learnt to keep my mouth shut, that I'd be savvy enough to know a chat with a local radio station could end up anywhere. That three-minute conversation caused ructions. The press pilloried me for being ungrateful. My manager, David Samuel, was one of many people who said I needed to watch what I said in future. I truly hadn't meant any harm. I was actually having a great time on S*plash!* Yes, the diving frightened the living daylights out of me, but on the plus side I was working with some fantastic people. Donna Air, Caprice and Linda Barker were lovely, proper women's women; Omid Djalili was hysterical. I got on with Eddie 'the Eagle' Edwards, Dom Joly, Anthony Ogogo, all of them. It was a great bunch.

I was diving in the third heat and really didn't expect to go through. My urticaria, was bad, but luckily you couldn't see it on TV. I was so sure I was going home I didn't even practise a dive for the following week.

'This is for Simon Turner,' I said, as I got ready to launch myself off the diving board.

Everyone was going, 'Who's Simon Turner?'

When I got voted through I couldn't believe it. More rescheduling for Simon Turner. Poor lad must have been cursing.

I shot my final scene for *Shameless* in my pink dressing gown in the Jockey. It wasn't a big storyline for Mimi. She was just there in the pub, being vile to Billy (Michael Taylor), as usual. I knew it would be emotional and didn't want any fuss. We did the scene, cut, and I saw Jean Holdsworth coming through the bar towards us. Michael was already in tears and I burst out crying. I managed a few words, thanked everyone, said how much I appreciated them, and then I ran down the corridor, pulled out my hair extensions for the last time, and had a good cry with Rachael, my make-up artist.

The next time I did *Splash!* I was up against Linda Barker in the dive-off and the judges sent me home. I can't tell you how relieved I was. Paul and I got in a car and went straight from the pool in Luton to Manchester for the *Shameless* wrap party. On the way, I got so many texts congratulating me, my phone jammed. The one from Dannielle made the whole *Splash!* nightmare worthwhile. *You looked stunning xxx.*

That was one I was going to keep.

A few weeks after we finished filming *Shameless*, I went into the studios at Wythenshawe to pack up my dressing room. That was hard. Over the years I'd made it homely with lots of personal touches and had photos of my family up, cruci-fixes, books, candles – lots of stuff I'd accumulated over the years. It was emotional putting everything into boxes, know-ing it was the last time I'd be there.

32

After months of juggling hectic work commitments, I was at last ready to get things moving with the IVF. On my fiftieth birthday, 30 January 2013, Paul and I went to see Mr Gazvani at the clinic in Rodney Street, signed all the papers, and agreed to start the treatment four weeks later on 1 March. It would involve travelling to Cyprus, where egg donors remain anonymous, unlike in the UK. That was important to me. If I was lucky enough to have a child, I didn't want someone turning up on the doorstep eighteen years later claiming to be its mother. Paul and I were so happy, on the brink of something that could turn out to be amazing. If all went to plan, life would never be the same again. I had every confidence in Mr Gazvani and was in no doubt we were in the best possible hands.

We decided to limit ourselves to three attempts at IVF, which seemed reasonable. If I didn't get pregnant, we would let it go. Even with the best treatment available, I was well aware it might not work. The clinic's success rate for a woman my age using donor eggs was a little over 60 per cent, which was good but far from certain, and what I didn't want was to become obsessed, wanting a baby at any cost, trying over and over, and having to cope with a series of disappointments. I had seen what that could do to couples and knew it wouldn't be good for me or Paul. I was already blessed with one child and was grateful for Dannielle. If I didn't get pregnant, it wouldn't be the end of the world. Paul felt the same.

For my fiftieth, I was having a party at the Carriageworks Hotel in Liverpool. Once we'd completed the paperwork at the clinic, we asked Mr Gazvani if he wanted to join us for a glass of champagne, but it turned out it was his wedding anniversary and he already had a celebration of his own planned. Usually, when it's my birthday it's like a parade, completely over the top. The celebrations go on all week. I have a party, a family night, a couples' night, a girly night. I want flowers and champagne (even though I don't drink), bows and balloons, charms for my bracelet. My cards stay up a month, at least. I'm like a child. I think it's because I never had that kind of fuss when I was little, so now I'm making up for it. This time, though, I kept it low key, about eighty people, family and friends. I wasn't in the mood to go mad or do a magazine deal and invite hundreds of guests from London and Manchester.

We went back to the hotel to get ready. After the stress of the panto and *Splash!* and *Shameless*, all I wanted to do was relax. The urticaria that had been plaguing me had cleared up. My weight had dropped to 8 stone 3 pounds and I was wearing size 8 clothes. People kept telling me I'd got too thin, but I felt great. I couldn't decide what to wear and narrowed it down to two dresses, a green and white fitted Missoni and a strappy black and green Cavalli. In the end, I started the night in the Cavalli and changed into the Missoni halfway through. I had a wonderful time surrounded by the people I cared most about. More than three years had passed since my aunty Doreen had been diagnosed with ovarian cancer, and she had been through three bouts of gruelling chemotherapy, which had helped give her more time but had also taken it out of her. She was very poorly and it was touch and go whether she'd be well enough to make the party but, luckily, she was having a good week and not only got there but was on the dance floor with me half the night.

On 1 March 2013, I started my first course of IVF. For the next few weeks I would be taking hormones, getting my body ready for pregnancy, all being well. Mr Gazvani told us what to expect.

'You will have mood swings, feel up and down, emotional, a bit strange,' he said.

'No change there, then,' Paul said.

For the first four weeks, I was on tablets that had to be taken at set times of the day. Then I went on to pessaries and twice-daily injections. I know lots of women don't like the injections, but I was fine with them. After years of injecting insulin for my diabetes, needles didn't bother me. Actually, Paul gave me the jabs, which kept him involved in the whole process.

I did feel emotional and strange, but I wasn't sure it was entirely down to the drugs. There was a lot of other stuff happening at the time. My aunty Doreen had been admitted to the Liverpool Women's Hospital and was at the stage where there was nothing more they could do for her in terms of treatment. It was heartbreaking. I went in to see her as much as I could. Everybody was distraught. I don't think any of us were ready to say goodbye, but on 22 March 2013, it was time to let her go. I'm not good with death, don't handle it well at all. When a drama student of mine, Rose Farley, who was fifteen, died in May 2012, after a bad ecstasy tablet, it was shocking, terrible. Her dad, Chris, was a good friend, I was close to her mum, Lynn, and really wanted to be at the funeral, but at the last minute on the day I couldn't manage it. With my dad, I went into the funeral home every day and spent time with him. With Doreen, I couldn't face going. I'm not sure what's worse, a sudden death, which was what happened with my dad, or an illness that means there's time to prepare for losing the person you love. Either way, it's incredibly hard. I was grateful for the time I had with Doreen in her final weeks, but I really didn't feel that knowing she was nearing the end of her life made it at all easier for any of us to cope when she died.

We had to wait until after Easter to have Doreen's funeral. It was held on 8 April 2013, at St Bede's church, in Widnes, and so many people turned up some had to stand outside. I did the eulogy and struggled to hold it together. Doreen was eighteen and Rob was sixteen when they met and they'd been together ever since. There was less than a year between Doreen and my mum and they'd been close all their lives.

Seeing my mother and Rob so upset, and thinking about how they were going to keep going without her, broke my heart. After losing my dad, I also knew how bad it was for our Lynn and Carol, who were like sisters to me, to lose their mum.

A couple of weeks later, on Wednesday 24 April, Paul and I flew to Cyprus for the next stage of the IVF process. We had Liz Santos and a film crew from ITV's *This Morning* with us. Purely by coincidence, Mr Gazvani and Jemma were on the same flight, sitting behind us, heading out to Cyprus for a seminar on IVF. For me, the trip was as much a break and a chance to get some sunshine as anything. I can honestly say I had no expectations. I told myself it was only the first attempt, so no point getting our hopes up. Whatever happened, Paul and I would get some time together.

We checked into the Arkin Palm Hotel, in Famagusta, and went for something to eat, had a quiet night. We didn't talk endlessly about what was going to happen in the coming days, just did our best to relax. I think we both felt it wasn't wise to pin our hopes on having success at the first attempt. The next morning we woke to blue skies and sunshine and went to the clinic to meet Dr Tekin, who'd be handling our treatment there. He talked us through what would happen next. We'd chosen a twenty-two-year-old classics graduate to be our donor and, although it's impossible to be exact about how many eggs you'll get, the clinic guaranteed we'd have at least ten. In fact, we got eighteen, which was wonderful.

The following day, Paul went in to give his sperm. Again, the clinic warned us it was unlikely all the eggs would be fertilized. 'If you end up with ten out of eighteen, you'll be doing really well,' Dr Tekin said. Paul only went and fertilized fifteen. You should have seen him, Johnny Big Balls. He was made up! Again, we were told to expect about half of them to be good, viable embryos. We actually had ten. So all the way through, things were going well, better than expected. It seemed a good sign. Still, we didn't get carried away.

We had a long way to go.

On Sunday 28 April, we went into the clinic to have two embryos implanted in my womb. The procedure was painless and over in a few minutes. With Paul holding my hand, we watched the monitor at the side of bed as the embryos, two tiny little dots, travelled up and into my womb. Both of us were quite tearful and then elated. Whatever happened next was in the lap of the gods. There was nothing more either of us could do. From then on, it was a waiting game.

We spent the rest of the day on the beach, sunbathing, going in the sea. I was the most relaxed I could be. The sadness I'd felt since Doreen had died seemed to ease. I thought about what a baby would mean, not just for me and Paul, but for the whole family, and said a prayer. On the beach, gazing out to sea, I wondered if Doreen was watching over me. I liked to think so. I was sure my dad was. I felt something on my arm and when I looked it was a ladybird. That made me smile. *Frank*. When I was little, my dad would always pick up a single ladybird and put it on me, and every time I saw one I thought of him. Beside me, Paul was stretched out in the sun. I gave him a nudge.

'Look at this,' I said, showing him my arm. 'Frank's here.'

The next morning I felt sick. I wasn't worried. I thought maybe I'd been more stressed about everything than I thought and it had churned me up. We went to the beach and had a lovely day. When I woke up the following day I felt different, *pregnant*. It was far too early to know, of course, but the feeling was real. I told Paul, half expecting him to tell me not to be daft, but he didn't.

'I really think you are,' he said.

We were under strict instructions from the clinic not to do a pregnancy test for at least ten days. Any earlier and we could get a false negative result. Apparently, in the early stages of pregnancy the hormone levels are low and it's possible to get a negative reading even if you're pregnant. For women undergoing IVF, it's not unheard of for them to be so disappointed and so stressed thinking it hasn't worked and they're not pregnant – when in fact they *are* – they end up miscarrying. At home, all we could think about was whether or not I was actually pregnant. A week after the embryos were implanted, my best mate, Kerry, came round. The tension was unbearable.

'I think you should just do a test and get it over with,' she said. 'I'll go and get one.'

I looked at Paul. 'I'm stressing anyway,' I said. 'I don't suppose a test can make things worse.'

He was getting ready to go to the gym. 'I'll go and get you one,' he said.

When he came back I disappeared into the loo. A couple of minutes later, I was in the living room clutching the little plastic wand. 'So, what happens next?' I said.

'It'll tell you in the window,' Kerry said.

I peered at it. 'How do you know if it's ready?' I gave it a shake, as if that would speed things up. Paul was pacing about behind me. I had another look at the little window. 'If it says "pregnant" does that mean I'm . . . *pregnant?*'

Paul threw his arms round me. Kerry jumped up and gave the pair of us a hug. All three of us were crying. I swore Kerry to secrecy and the next morning phoned Jemma at the UK CFA clinic in Liverpool and told her what I'd done. 'I know we shouldn't have, but we just couldn't wait,' I said.

'OK, wait another five days and repeat the test,' she said.

Another five days! No way could I wait that long. Over the next few days I did another three tests and each one was positive. *I* was positive. I was definitely pregnant.

I phoned my mum and told her the news. She was shocked, very emotional. I don't think she expected me to get pregnant at the first attempt. In all honesty, I didn't either. I really thought it would be the second or even third attempt – *if* I was lucky. In my wildest dreams, I never imagined it working first time. I think that's why everybody was so thrown by the news. The general reaction of people was gobsmacked. I'd been talking about having a baby and thinking about IVF on and off for a few years, ever since I'd met Paul, and all of a sudden I was pregnant, although it was very early days. Once the news sank in, Mum was ecstatic.

Although Dannielle knew about the IVF, telling her I was pregnant was the hardest thing in the world. Besides Paul, she was the person who was going to be most affected by me having another child. I wanted her to know that what she and I had was unique, that I could never repeat what we shared. I grew up with Dannielle. What we went through together was special. I could never emulate it. Looking back, I was a kid when I had her, even though I thought I was all grown up, and, while the circumstances around my pregnancy weren't happy, having her was an absolute joy, the best thing that had happened to me. I had been bowled over by her and would sit and look at her for hours. Everything about her fascinated me. I could never have another child as much like me as Dannielle. She's funny, bright, intelligent, beautiful . . . and she can be a little witch! She is the little girl with the curl from the nursery rhyme, the one who when she's bad is horrid, or, as Dannielle would say, 'When I'm bad, I'm better!' I suppose the way I felt about her reflected what I'd gone through to have her. This time was a different kettle of fish in every way. I was older, in a settled, happy marriage. Everything had changed.

Two weeks later, Paul and I went to see Mr Gazvani and got a telling-off. 'You're very naughty. I told you to wait,' he said. I told him how I'd had the most bizarre feeling I was pregnant within a couple of days of the embryos going in and that the urge to find out for sure that Sunday night after coming home from Cyprus was too much.

He seemed surprised we'd done the test in the evening. Apparently, so early into a pregnancy you should only really get a positive reading in the morning. 'That tells me the hormone levels are strong, and to me that indicates twins,' he said.

At five weeks' pregnant, we went for a scan at the Rodney Street clinic. I'd had a bit of bleeding but wasn't panicking. I knew it could happen in the early stages of pregnancy and didn't necessarily mean there was anything to worry about. Mr Gazvani was right. The scan clearly showed both embryos. It was amazing, the best news Paul and I could have hoped for. Both of us were in tears, overjoyed, but it was short-lived. Within a few minutes, it was obvious that only one of the embryos had actually survived. The bleeding I'd had was probably a sign of me losing the other one. I'm not being heartless, but I wasn't devastated. I didn't feel as if I'd lost a baby. It was too soon in the whole process and it seemed to me that it was just one of those things, not meant to be.

With my pregnancy confirmed, I had my first appointment at the antenatal clinic at the Liverpool Women's Hospital. It seemed poignant that a few months before I'd been there to see my aunty Doreen at the end of her life. Now, I was bringing another baby into the family. With Dannielle, I had morning sickness for the first twelve weeks. With this baby I was sick as a dog but not actually throwing up. I felt nauseous, on and off, all the time. The sickness came in waves and there was no relief from it. I tried walking about but it didn't help. Lying down made no difference. I was going to have to live with it. At times I felt so sick I could have cried, but at the same time I was that excited about the baby, nothing could dent my mood. At the hospital, I was told my sickness was a good sign because it meant my pregnancy hormone levels were high, which made me feel better – not literally, unfortunately!

33

I had Dannielle at eighteen and there I was, pregnant again at fifty. First time round, I knew nothing. In lots of ways it was that much simpler. There was very little advice, so I ate what I wanted to eat, carried on having a drink. Nobody said to stop smoking and drinking or that I shouldn't be going on sunbeds. This time there was so much to take in, dos and don'ts – it was overwhelming. It seemed that almost every day there was something else to worry about – petrol fumes, hairspray, body products . . . I tried to find a happy medium and not become paranoid. The last thing I wanted was to get too caught up in all the baby books, because it could drive you mad trying to take on board all the advice that's out there. The worst thing for the baby was for its mother to get stressed, was how I felt.

When I was eighteen I hardly saw the inside of an antenatal clinic. As an older mother, there seemed to be much more vigilance. I was in and out of clinics all the time, and under the care of the Medical Disorders Unit of the Liverpool Women's Hospital, purely because at my age there was a greater risk of complications. It felt strange because I didn't feel like I had any health issues. My blood pressure was fine. When I had my lung function test it was excellent. All my blood tests showed there was nothing to worry about. The only concern was that my iron levels were low and, as I've always been prone to anaemia, that came as no surprise. I really don't like liver but I almost bought some, thinking it's such a good source of iron it might be an idea to get some inside me, then the nurse at the antenatal clinic said you're not allowed to have it when you're pregnant because it's high in vitamin A and that's not good for the baby. Yet another thing I didn't know about. They put me on ferrous sulphate tablets three times a day to boost my iron, aspirin to keep my blood thin, and I was already taking a pregnancy multi-vitamin.

Five tablets a day, as opposed to the twenty-eight I was on for IVF.

I was trying to eat as well as I could – spinach and broccoli and lots of fresh vegetables. Feeling so sick meant that a lot of the time all I was able to stomach were a couple of mouthfuls of cereal. Honey Nut Loops, Rice Krispies, Coco Pops, Frosties, Crunchy Nut Cornflakes. I started buying the variety packs so, when I couldn't decide what to have, I mixed up a couple of different ones. I found there was something very comforting about a bowl of cornflakes with ice-cold milk in the early hours of the morning when I was up ironing or baking or making one of my lists. Then, of course, I read somewhere that cereal is full of sugar and rubbish and isn't good for you . . .

When I was expecting Dannielle, the only craving I had was for pickled onions. I could sit and eat a whole jar. This time, to my absolute horror, when I was a few weeks pregnant, I had a sudden craving for a kebab. I don't even like kebabs. I never eat them. I'm usually such a snob about food these days and buy the best of everything – organic chicken, tons of spinach, fish. But this particular night I had to have a kebab. The works. Where we live, in a pretty village on the outskirts of Manchester, there's no such thing as a takeaway. I actually think there's a local by-law against kebab shops and what-have-you – seriously. Paul had to get in the car and go looking for one. It was the first kebab I'd had in years and, to my amazement, I thoroughly enjoyed it. I ate loads of it. Thankfully, the kebab craving only lasted a couple of weeks before I went right off them. The last one I had, I only managed a tiny amount and Bella got the rest.

On 22 July 2013, me and Paul went to see Mr Gazvani for a scan. I was nearly fifteen weeks pregnant. It was unbelievable to see how much the baby was moving, flipping over and waving her arms. No wonder I was nauseous with all that going on inside me. We could make out her eyes, her nose, her mouth, and, oh my God, the heartbeat was incredible. I say 'her' because I was already sure I was having a girl, even though it was impossible to know at that stage.

From the outset, when I'd seen Mr Kingsland, I was told that if I was fortunate enough to get pregnant, I would need a Caesarean delivery because of my age. 'Book it at the point of conception,' he said, which made absolute sense to me. The last thing I wanted was to take any unnecessary risks. Seventeen weeks into my pregnancy, no one had spoken to me about delivery until I saw a young female doctor at the antenatal clinic in the Women's Hospital. Paul was with me. The doctor read through my notes. 'How are you feeling?'

'I'm really well. They've checked my pulse, temperature, blood pressure, and everything's fine,' I said.

She didn't look up. 'You're aware you're at an increased risk of having a baby with spina bifida or Down's syndrome because of your age,' she said.

I glanced at Paul. 'The thing is, my egg donor was twenty-two years of age and I've been told that means the risk is a lot less than if I'd used my own eggs.'

'Oh, it's an IVF baby.' There was something offhand about the way she said it.

I told her about seeing Mr Kingsland, being referred to the clinic in Rodney Street for treatment.

'You'll already know your due date, then, you don't need me to tell you,' she said.

'So, I'll be having a caesarean, that's what I've been advised,' I said. 'Only no one's discussed it with me or talked about a birthing plan or anything.'

'There's no need for a caesarean. You're fit and healthy for your age, so I don't see why you shouldn't have a normal delivery.'

Paul didn't look happy at all. I couldn't work out why this young doctor was being so dismissive. This was massively important to us. We were expecting our first child together and wanted to make sure everything went smoothly.

'It's just, when I saw your top gynaecologist privately – in this hospital – he told me to book my caesarean as soon as I got pregnant,' I said.

She gave me the kind of look that was hard to read. Not friendly, that much was obvious. 'There's no reason whatsoever for that,' she said. 'We'll be in touch about your next appointment.'

We left her office in a bit of a daze and feeling upset. I couldn't help wondering whether she disapproved of us having IVF; maybe thought I was too old to be having a baby.

Paul was furious. 'You're having a caesarean and that's that,' he said.

My mum was in no doubt what was going on. caesarean births cost more than normal deliveries. 'It's about the money,' she said.

Having paid National Insurance contributions all my life – in excess of £300 a week at times – I felt entitled to give birth by whatever means was best for me *and* the baby. I took to Twitter to find out what other women had to say. Should I have the right to opt for a caesarean if that was what I felt comfortable with, even if it cost more? I was inundated with replies and the overwhelming feeling was that it was *my* body, *my* choice. Before long, someone from the Women's Hospital was in touch. I said I wasn't after special treatment, but as an older mother I didn't want to take any chances, and I was assured that whatever kind of birth I wanted, it was up to me and they would do all they could to support me. I could only think the doctor we saw must have been having an off day.

I knew that some people felt fifty was too old to be having a baby. It really didn't bother me. I was fitter and healthier than I was at thirty and had gone to great lengths to get my body ready for pregnancy. I'd heard all the arguments about how I'd be sixty when my child was ten, but I really didn't see a problem there. I looked at my mother, seventy-four with an energetic lifestyle, going on holiday with my daughter of thirty-two, eating out, going to nightclubs, keeping up with a woman not even half her age. It was down to the individual, in my opinion. I knew people in their twenties who'd had children willy-nilly and couldn't cope. I also knew women who'd been middle-aged in their outlook from the age of twenty. I was fit and well, in a loving, secure relationship. As long as I could provide love, confidence, support, education, and a stable and loving home, why shouldn't I have a child?

Since I had my gastric band fitted and started losing weight, my diabetes had cleared up and I no longer had to inject insulin any more, although I did have to monitor my blood sugar levels carefully, as there was a chance of developing gestational diabetes. Because of a mix-up, I missed having the test that would normally have been done at twelve weeks for Down's syndrome and spina bifida, but I wasn't anxious. I wasn't exactly a typical older mother. A blood test I had later showed that I was in the lowest 20 per cent category in terms of risk. Nothing to worry about.

I was paranoid about putting on weight. Within the first few weeks I put on 2 stone, which seemed a lot to me. I went back to the Hospital Group and asked to have my gastric band tightened because I was worried about getting too big, but they wouldn't do it. I knew, of course, there was a perfectly good reason for gaining weight. I was pregnant, not a greedy pig, but I still didn't like getting bigger. I could feel it on my arms and on my back, and my boobs were the biggest they'd ever been and so sore. My problem was, I was thinking like a thin bird, so it wasn't a case of, 'Great, I'm pregnant, I'm going to eat.' I actually felt the opposite, that I didn't want to go mad. I was told you could put on anything from 3 to 5 stone during pregnancy. Four stone, tops, and I'd be happy.

I was feeling particularly fat, obviously nothing like I was, but still. And I was emotional, a bit weepy. Paul was great, giving me foot massages, making me feel better. When he said, 'You're absolutely beautiful to me,' I knew he meant it. I was very lucky to have found him so late in the game. It was brilliant to be in love, to have someone who cared, who would die for you; to have no doubts whatsoever about them always being there for you. Just lovely.

He was going to make a great dad.

Epilogue

I was all geared up to have the baby by Caesarean on New Year's Eve, 2013. In the run-up to the birth I was as busy as ever, filming a documentary and hosting my regular weekly pub quiz night at Ma Egerton's. I'd also started doing another quiz at a pub in Ormskirk, the Eureka. I was getting really tired, drained, and needed an afternoon nap to keep going, which wasn't like me at all. I got incredibly frustrated at not being able to summon the energy to do the things I was used to doing. It felt like a weakness to me. Then, in early December, I started feeling poorly – headachy, as if I'd been wearing a hat that was too tight and was digging into my skull. I kept saying I felt fine when I didn't really. Finally, I told my midwife my head was hurting and she told me to go to the doctor. I got an appointment first thing the next morning – Friday, 13 December. The night before, I was at the Eureka hosting the quiz with an aching head and blurred vision. My legs had swollen up as well. I was really quite ill.

I got ready for the doctor's and did my make-up, thinking Paul and I could go to John Lewis afterwards and pick up some baby things. When the doctor checked my blood pressure it was up. What with that and the state of my legs, he suspected pre-eclampsia, a complication in pregnancy that can prove fatal. I was going to have to go straight to the Women's Hospital.

'They won't keep me in, will they?' I said, thinking about all the baby stuff we still needed to get.

At the hospital I was taken to the emergency department and hooked up to a monitor to see how the baby was doing. She was fine, but I wasn't so good – my blood pressure was going crazy. For the next few hours nurses and midwives and doctors came and went, monitoring me and the baby, taking blood, testing my urine. They were so vigilant, couldn't do enough. I could see Paul getting anxious, but what was strange was that I felt completely calm, nothing like I'd been in recent months when I was crying my eyes out over nothing. After something like six hours a consultant confirmed it *was* pre-eclampsia and they were keeping me in overnight. Even then, I was running through lists of things to do once I got home. Paul nipped out to get me some pyjamas and spent the night on a mattress at the side of my bed.

The next day, I had a bit of bleeding and so I was kept in again, and I settled down for a second night in hospital. Every couple of hours, my blood pressure was checked. Usually it's 110 over 50 but it was up as high as 185 over 100. My legs were massive and something weird had happened to my face. It had gone enormous and completely changed shape. That was the pre-eclampsia. A consultant came in and said it was likely they'd deliver the baby in the next few days. All I could think was that I had a big family party planned a few days later and didn't want to let everyone down. We still needed loads of baby things too, including a car seat. Mrs Organised, that's me – and I hadn't even packed my hospital bag. A couple of hours later the consultant was back to say I'd be having the baby the following day, no ifs or buts.

On Sunday, 15 December, I went into theatre, still with a headache, feeling pretty rotten. They gave me a spinal block anaesthetic to numb my lower body. It was surreal, being conscious and about to be operated on, and looking up at the medical team in their gowns and masks. As they prepared to make the incision, Paul held my hand. I was hooked up to a blood-pressure monitor and suddenly, someone said, 'Have you seen that?' I heard whispering. Apparently, my blood pressure was sky high, 220 over 100. I had no idea how serious things were but Paul did and it frightened the life out of him. He thought he might lose me.

I felt the incision, the consultant tugging at my insides and heard the midwife say what a wonderful head of hair the baby had ... then we heard her cry. It was 1.42 p.m. I broke down and Paul sobbed as they put our daughter in my arms, still bloody and covered in gunk. Tears streamed down my face as I held her.

She was beautiful, perfect, the image of Paul. At 6lbs 7oz, she was a good weight, especially for a premature baby, but she was slightly jaundiced and went straight to the special-care unit into a cot with a heat pad. She had a feeding tube up her nose, a drip in her hand, and it broke my heart to see them take blood from her tiny heel to check her sugar levels.

Paul and I sat with her for hours. That first night I couldn't stop crying. I wanted to feed her myself but she wasn't sucking hard enough so I expressed my milk and gave her it in a bottle with some Aptimil formula. She was so tiny and fragile-looking I was nervous about picking her up. I couldn't do it. Paul was better than me and did the first nappy change and changed her clothes.

We'd picked a name well before the baby was born: Flame. That raised a few eyebrows! When I told Mum and Aunty Val they looked at me as if I was insane. For a long time Paul and I liked Darcey or Fleur, until we saw nine-year-old Flame Brewer on the news doing a wing walk to raise money for charity. We turned to each other at the same time and exclaimed, 'Flame!' We loved it and the more I thought about it, the more perfect it felt. (When I said, 'Oh my God, she started life as a tiny idea, a *flame* in our hearts,' Paul rolled his eyes.) Flame Frances Josephine Malone. Frances after my mum, Olwyn Frances and my dad Frank and Josephine after my nan and my Aunty Doreen – it was her middle name.

After three days in the special-care unit we got her back and a couple of days later went home. That night, I sat up in the living room wrapped in a quilt watching my daughter, utterly mesmerised, as she lay in her Moses basket. I was thinking about my dad, wishing he was there, knowing he was watching over us. I could not take my eyes off my baby or get over how good she was. She smiled, had her feed, hiccupped, laughed, slept ... honest to God, she never cried. Paul and I took it in turns with her feeds through the night and less than a week after coming home, we celebrated our first Christmas as a family. For once, Paul and I hadn't gone mad on presents; aftershave for him, perfume for me. All that mattered was we'd got the baby we'd dreamed of. Our only sadness was that on Christmas night my mum's cousin, Rosemary, who'd been ill with breast cancer, died.

All through my pregnancy, my mother was amazing. Back in April 2013, when I began the IVF process, not long after my Aunty Doreen died, Mum was grieving and in a bad way. If you'd asked her then how she felt about me having IVF at fifty I think she'd have said she'd rather I didn't but the baby brought the two of us closer than we've been for years. Dannielle was besotted too, determined to turn her little sister into a Disney princess.

Thinking back to when I had Dannielle at eighteen, going through it on my own, this time round things could not have been more different, with Paul there every step of the way, my hospital room crammed with family and friends, so many balloons and gifts you could hardly get through the door.

I meant what I said about not minding the sleepless nights. I'm exhausted but exhilarated. I'd go and do it all again tomorrow but Paul says not a chance – it's too risky, so we'll see if I can talk him round.

All the soul-searching we did about using a donor egg was not the least bit important in the end, especially as new research suggests the baby also gets DNA from the placenta – which may explain why my mum is convinced Flame has my nose.

It's a new year and I'd usually be making one of my lists of things to do in 2014 but for once I'm in no hurry. I've already done the biggest thing of all – had my baby against the odds.

Our little miracle, Flame

January 2014